LITERARY COMPANION TO
THE LECTIONARY

Literary Companion

TO THE

Lectionary

———◇———

A Poetic Gathering
to Accompany the Readings
for Sundays, Principal Feasts and
Selected Holy Days

Compiled and edited by

Mark Pryce

Fortress Press
Minneapolis

For Peter Walker, Bishop:

companion, counsellor and interpreter of poets

LITERARY COMPANION TO THE LECTIONARY

First Fortress Press edition 2002

Cover design: Andrea Rossi
Cover graphic: 'Canticum Canticorum' by Eric Gill
Book design and typesetting: Kenneth Burnley, Wirral, Cheshire, England

ISBN 0-8006-3464-0

Manufactured in Great Britain   1-3464

05 04 03 02 1 2 3 4 5 6 7 8 9 10

CONTENTS

FOREWORD

Reading the Bible through the year in eucharist and office is something that is meant to feed our imagination, so that, time after time, we rediscover with a bit of a shock what Clement of Alexandria called 'the freshness of grace'. But we'd all admit, I expect, that it is not always so; readings slip by, the most outrageous and wonderful things become usual to us. And it's at this point above all that we need one another, that we need to read together.

Reading together is what Christians have always done, of course; even the much-maligned sermon is (or ought to be) an attempt to share the experience of Scripture. There will always be people who have been reading the Bible before we started on it, and we need their perceptions and perspectives. But across the centuries, the response to the biblical narrative has been not just in prayer and sermon and theology, but in poetry and meditative prose. And what this book attempts is to let us read together with those who have allowed their imaginations to be kindled into creativity by our common story of salvation.

Some of these texts may be familiar, but I think that the majority will be new to many readers. Mark Pryce has drawn upon a wonderfully broad range of material. Here the English metaphysical poets stand alongside modern writers. There are great theologians – Gregory Dix, William Vanstone – off-duty, as you might say, showing us exactly why theology was their meat and drink. There are people – Thomas Hardy, Dorothy Parker, Albert Camus, George Steiner – who are not at all 'the usual suspects' for an anthology on the Christian year, people whose insight and compassion are revelatory enough for them to be proper witnesses to the revealed story almost in spite of themselves.

It has been a joy to make the acquaintance of this particular cloud of witnesses. Mark Pryce offers a real education in reading alongside a company of people whose love of words opens up a new level of love for the Word – the Word made flesh, the Word of witness in Scripture. Time spent in this company is – if you'll forgive the liturgical pun – a good deal more than just Ordinary Time.

ROWAN WILLIAMS

INTRODUCTION

The worship of God is at the heart of Christian community and discipleship. Though God is ultimately beyond description, and prays within us at a spiritual level deeper than words (cf. Romans 8.26), the self-expression of God in Christ calls forth the gift of language from within us in an outpouring of praise: our lives are lived in thankful response to the Co-creating Word made flesh. Divine worship is a response in words, and finds its fullest expression in the words of the liturgy of the Eucharist. In liturgy the world is opened up to the divine in thanksgiving, and in this celebration our vision of God, of our selves and our fellow creatures is renewed through the eye of praise. Worship seeks to engage the whole human being, transforming our entire selves and our sense of all creation. The power and creativity of the imagination is essential in this opening up and renewal of perception, of re-visioning in wonder, thanksgiving and compassion. In building a bridge between literature and liturgy the intention of this Companion is to prompt imaginative engagement in worship and study of the Scriptures through writings which affirm or re-work, or even challenge, themes emerging out of the words of Bible texts and liturgical prayer.

Literature helps us pay attention to the world and to the experience of its creatures and to the work of its Creator, Redeemer and Sustainer God. In this way it can nourish prayer and inspire praise. The poet, novelist and playwright help us bring the world into our worship, and to recognize the divine at play in the world – not only the natural world, but also the world of the city and of human relationships. These words in literary forms can be the gateway to contemplation: resting our attention on the Word present in specific persons or places, the one who is always beyond and never contained by them. Literature traces in our lives and the life of the world the glory and presence of the living and active God of whom the words of liturgy and Scripture speak. Les Murray writes that a poem is 'an afterlife on earth', the recognition of the divine immanence which George Herbert calls 'heaven in ordinarie'. R. S. Thomas celebrates the 'tree of poetry' as 'eternity wearing the green leaves of time'.

Yet God remains a hidden God, indescribable, one who is clouded in the dark light of unknowing. A poet such as R. S. Thomas or a writer such as Tolstoy speaks of this God too: of God's absence from human experience, God's distance from the human heart, God's inscrutability to the human mind. This mystical yearning and search for the elusive divine is part of the human spiritual journey – a journey which passes through doubt as well as faith – and in which this very hiddenness becomes an aspect of God's compelling beauty.

The writers' expressions of faith or doubt represented here encourage not only a deeper consideration of the things of God, but also of our own lives and feelings. In this way too literature helps the words of worship take on an amplified sense, for in keeping company with a variety of performative, narrative or poetic texts which speak out of a range of different cultures and historical contexts, we glimpse our own shifting createdness and creativity. Represented here are varieties of faith and doubt springing from a diversity of people and places – what Brendan Kennelly has called 'a parliament of voices'. In this sense the material gathered here reminds us that Religion is Poetry: that is, something made of words in response to a person or idea or experience, given form and expression and approximated within the limits of language, ideology and culture. Religious language is full of images, analogies and narratives which can come alive in a new way when set among imaginative writings such as these. Read in the fresh light of literary imagination, the literature of Scripture becomes a greater delight and a greater challenge for our lives. When our imagination is hampered or impoverished, then our prayer is cramped and our interpretation is shallow. Hence this is a book which aims for richer meanings and deepened understandings, to ward off spiritual stagnation and the withering of compassion.

On a practical note, readers will see from the table of contents that this book offers poems and literary pieces for Sundays, Principal Feasts and Holy Days in the Liturgical Year. Each selection relates to an aspect of the Scripture readings given for the Eucharist in the Revised Common Lectionary. The brief introductory notes which preface each literary selection sometimes draw out a theme in the Scriptures which seems to thread across the three-year cycle, but more frequently suggests the literary text as a response to an idea, image or story found in a single biblical reading or seasonal theme. Where selections relate to readings for the special Church of England provisions, these are marked with an asterisk★.

Given the character of the Lectionary, on some Sundays in some years readers will draw blanks, but for the most part there is enough from which reflection can arise and ideas grow. Bearing in mind the vast tradition of literature in English, inevitably individual readers are bound to come across absences which will seem to them unhappy omissions. For this great literary wealth I cannot apologize, except to say that I am sorry there is not space here to include more of it. The selection is deliberately eclectic and ecumenical, and goes beyond explicitly Christian writers where appropriate. The selection is intended to provide material, direct or indirect, for sermons and teaching, and to be a starting point for meditation and prayer. Given the nature of language, not all the selected pieces will be immediately meaningful or relevant to all persons at all times; some will require patience and hard work, and others – as always in literary appreciation – might be better left for another day.

I am grateful to the people who have assisted me in the work of gathering and editing material for this collection, and among them especially Fr Michael Bowie, Dr Helen Hewson, Professor Leslie Houlden, Dr Anna Lawrence, Professor Linne Mooney, Canon David Peacock, Fr Sam Portarro, and Dr James Woodward. I am also grateful to the people of Christ Church St Laurence, Sydney, and the Warden and Fellows of St Paul's College, Sydney, for their hospitality during the compiling of the *Companion*, and to Ruth McCurry of SPCK for her patient guidance and support.

MARK PRYCE
Corpus Christi College, Cambridge

SUNDAYS,
PRINCIPAL FEASTS
AND HOLY DAYS

THE FIRST SUNDAY OF ADVENT

————◄○►————

From *Old And New Year Ditties*

Christina Rossetti, English, 1830–94

Rossetti's poem is an assent to some key Advent themes: mortality, watchfulness, patience, and final consummation.

Passing away, saith the World, passing away:
Chances, beauty, and youth, sapped day by day:
Thy life never continueth in one stay.
Is the eye waxen dim, is the dark hair changing to grey
That hath won neither laurel nor bay?
I shall clothe myself in Spring and bud in May:
Thou, root-stricken, shall not rebuild thy decay
On my bosom for aye.
Then I answered: Yea.

Passing away, saith my Soul, passing away:
With its burden of fear and hope, of labour and play,
Hearken what the past doth witness and say:
Rust in thy gold, a moth is in thy array,
A canker is in thy bud, thy leaf must decay.
At midnight, at cockcrow, at morning, one certain day
Lo, the Bridegroom shall come and shall not delay;
Watch thou and pray.
Then I answered: Yea.

Passing away, saith my God, passing away:
Winter passeth after the long delay:
New grapes on the vine, new figs on the tender spray,
Turtle calleth turtle in Heaven's May.
Though I tarry, wait for Me, trust Me, watch and pray:
Arise, come away, night is past and lo it is day,
My love, My sister, My spouse, thou shalt hear Me say.
Then I answered: Yea.

THE SECOND SUNDAY OF ADVENT

◄○►

Advent Calendar

Rowan Williams, Welsh, 1950–

Like the great prophet John the Baptist, here the poet proclaims the coming Christ who is Saviour and Judge.

> He will come like last leaf's fall.
> One night when the November wind
> has flayed the trees to bone, and earth
> wakes choking on the mould,
> the soft shroud's folding.
>
> He will come like frost.
> One morning when the shrinking earth
> opens on mist, to find itself
> arrested in the net
> of alien, sword-set beauty.
>
> He will come like dark.
> One evening when the bursting red
> December sun draws up the sheet
> and penny-masks its eye to yield
> the star-snowed fields of sky.
>
> He will come, will come,
> will come like crying in the night,
> like blood, like breaking,
> as the earth writhes to toss him free.
> He will come like child.

THE THIRD SUNDAY OF ADVENT

―――◄○►―――

The Darkling Thrush

Thomas Hardy, English, 1840–1928

Nature speaks a gospel which humans have forgotten: the joyful birdsong
in the bleak winter evening seems like a proclamation of hope.

I leant upon a coppice gate
    When Frost was spectre-gray,
And Winter's dregs made desolate
    The weakening eye of day.
The tangled bine-stems scored the sky
    Like strings of broken lyres,
And all mankind that haunted nigh
    Had sought their household fires.

The land's sharp features seem'd to be
    The Century's corpse outleant,
His crypt the cloudy canopy,
    The wind his death-lament.
The ancient pulse of germ and birth
    Was shrunken hard and dry,
And every spirit upon earth
    Seem'd fervourless as I.

At once a voice arose among
    The bleak twigs overhead
In a full-hearted evensong
    Of joy illimited;
An aged thrush, frail, gaunt, and small,
    In blast-beruffled plume,
Had chosen thus to fling his soul
    Upon the growing gloom.

So little cause for carollings
    Of such ecstatic sound
Was written on terrestrial things
    Afar or nigh around,
That I could think there trembled through
    His happy good-night air
Some blessed Hope, whereof he knew
    And I was unaware.

The Fourth Sunday of Advent

From *Three Poems of Incarnation*

Kathleen Raine, English, 1908–

In this mysterious poem a child stands on the threshold of life, of the home, of the human heart, and he is warned not to enter a place so full of pain. This is the Christ who comes to a world in desperate need of him, which feels itself unworthy of his love.

Who stands at my door in the storm and rain
On the threshold of being?
One who waits till you call him in
From the empty night.

Are you a stranger, out in the storm,
Or has my enemy found me out
On the edge of being?

I am no stranger who stands at the door
Nor enemy come in the secret night,
I am your child, in darkness and fear
On the verge of being.

Go back, my child, to the rain and the storm,
For in this house there is sorrow and pain
In the lonely night.

I will not go back for sorrow or pain,
For my true love weeps within
And waits for my coming.

Go back, my babe, to the vacant night
For in this house dwell sin and hate
On the verge of being.

I will not go back for hate or sin,
I will not go back for sorrow or pain,
For my true love mourns within
On the threshold of night.

CHRISTMAS DAY

———◄◦►———

From *The Nativity*, part of *The Mysteries*, adapted from medieval play cycles

Tony Harrison, English, 1937–

In this wonderful nativity scene three shepherds come to the infant Jesus and his mother with their presents of cherries, a pet bird and a ball. Their sheer delight in the child is adoration at its most authentic and profound.

1ST SHEPHERD
Hail, comely and clean!   Hail, young child!
Hail, maker, as I mean,   of maiden so mild!
Thou hast confounded, I ween,   the Warlock so wild:
The false bringer of teen,   now goes he beguiled.
    Lo, merry he is!
Lo, he laughs, my sweeting!
Ah! A very fair meeting!
I have held to my telling:
    Have a bob of cherries.

2ND SHEPHERD
Hail, sovereign saviour,   for thou hast us sought!
Hail, nurseling and flower,   that all thing has wrought!
Hail, full of favour,   that make all out of nought!
Hail! I kneel and I cower.   A bird have I brought
    To my bairn.
Hail, little tiny mop!
Of our creed thou art crop:
I would drink of thy cup,
    Little day-starne.

3RD SHEPHERD

Hail, little darling dear,   full of Godhead!
I pray thee be near   when that I have need.
Hail, sweet in thy cheer!   My heart will bleed
To see thee sit here   in so poor a weed,
     With no pennies.
Hail! Put forth thy dall.
I bring thee but a ball:
Have and play the withall,
     And go to the tennis.

MARY

The father of heaven,   God omnipotent,
That set all in days seven,   his son has he sent.
My name could he namen,   and on me his light spent!
I conceived him full even   by God's might as he meant;
     And now is he born.
May he keep you from woe!
I shall pray him so.
Tell forth as ye go,
     And mind on this morn.

THE FIRST SUNDAY OF CHRISTMAS

————◄○►————

Prayer for a New Mother

Dorothy Parker, American, 1893–1967

Dorothy Parker was famous for her acute and witty insights into human relationships. In this poignant verse she reflects on Mary's feelings as she treasures the extraordinary events of her son's birth and childhood, and ponders what they foretell of his painful destiny.

The things she knew, let her forget again –
   The voices in the sky, the fear, the cold,
The gaping shepherds, and the queer old men
   Piling their clumsy gifts of foreign gold.

Let her have laughter with her little one;
   Teach her the endless, tuneless songs to sing;
Grant her her right to whisper to her son
   The foolish names one dare not call a king.

Keep from her dreams the rumble of a crowd,
   The smell of rough-cut wood, the trail of red,
The thick and chilly whiteness of the shroud
   That wraps the strange new body of the dead.

Ah, let her go, kind Lord, where mothers go
   And boast his pretty words and ways, and plan
The proud and happy years that they shall know
   Together, when her son is grown a man.

THE SECOND SUNDAY OF CHRISTMAS

------◄◦►------

The Nativity of Our Lord and Saviour Jesus Christ, from *Hymns and Spiritual Songs* (No. 32)

Christopher Smart, English, 1722–71

Smart's exuberant lyric celebrates the Word made flesh.

> Where is this stupendous stranger,
>   Swains of Solyma, advise,
> Lead me to my Master's manger,
>   Show me where my Saviour lies?
>
> O MOST Mighty! O MOST HOLY!
>   Far beyond the Seraph's thought,
> Art thou then so mean and lowly
>   As unheeded prophets taught?
>
> O the magnitude of meekness!
>   Worth from worth immortal sprung;
> O the strength of infant weakness,
>   If eternal is so young!
>
> If so young and thus eternal,
>   Michael tune the Shepherd's reed,
> Where the scenes are ever vernal,
>   And the loves be love indeed!
>
> See the God blasphem'd and doubted
>   In the schools of Greece and Rome;
> See the powers of darkness routed,
>   Taken at their utmost gloom.

Nature's decorations glisten
    Far above their usual trim;
Birds on box and laurels listen,
    As so near the cherubs hymn.

Boreas now no longer winters
    On the desolated coast;
Oaks no more are riv'n in splinters
    By the whirlwind and his host.

Spinks and ouzles sing sublimely,
    'We too have a Saviour born,'
Whiter blossoms burst untimely
    On the blest Mosaic thorn.

God all-bounteous, all-creative,
    Whom no ills from good dissuade,
Is incarnate, and a native
    Of the very world he made.

THE EPIPHANY

Hymn

Sidney Godolphin, English, 1610–43

Here Godolphin compares the Magi to the Shepherds, and concludes that knowledge and expertise must take their proper place alongside wonder, love and other virtues before Christ.

Lord, when the wise men came from far,
Led to thy cradle by a star,
Then did the shepherds too rejoice,
Instructed by thy angel's voice.
Blest were the wise men in their skill,
And shepherds in their harmless will.

Wise men, in tracing Nature's laws,
Ascend unto the highest cause;
Shepherds with humble fearfulness
Walk safely, though their light be less.
Though wise men better know the way,
It seems no honest heart can stray.

There is no merit in the wise
But love, the shepherd's sacrifice.
Wise men, all ways of knowledge passed,
To the shepherd's wonder come at last.
To know can only wonder breed,
And not to know is wonder's seed.

A wise man at the altar bows,
And offers up his studied vows,
And is received. May not the tears,
Which spring too from a shepherd's fears,
And sighs upon his frailty spent,
Though not distinct, be eloquent?

'Tis true, the object sanctifies
All passions which within us rise,
But since no creature comprehends
The cause of causes, end of ends,
He who himself vouchsafes to know
Best pleases his creator so.

When then our sorrows we apply
To our own wants and poverty,
When we look up in all distress,
And our own misery confess,
Sending both thanks and prayers above,
Then, though we do not know, we love.

THE BAPTISM OF CHRIST
(THE FIRST SUNDAY OF EPIPHANY)

————◁◦▷————

The Coming

R. S. Thomas, Welsh, 1913–2000

At his Baptism Jesus is revealed as God's agent who comes in solidarity
with sinful humanity to bring restoration. Here the poet imagines Jesus
choosing his mission.

And God held in his hand
A small globe. Look, he said.
The son looked. Far off,
As through water, he saw
A scorched land of fierce
Colour. The light burned
There; crusted buildings
Cast their shadows; a bright
Serpent, a river
Uncoiled itself, radiant
With slime.
    On a bare
Hill a bare tree saddened
The sky. Many people
Held out their thin arms
To it, as though waiting
For a vanished April
To return to its crossed
Boughs. The son watched
Them. Let me go there, he said.

THE SECOND SUNDAY OF EPIPHANY

From *For the Time Being*

W. H. Auden, English, 1907–73

God's glory shines out in Jesus as he draws disciples (Gospel, Years A and B) – those who follow him, believe in him, and live their lives in the celebration of love which he inaugurates at Cana (Gospel, Year C).

He is the Way.
Follow Him through the Land of Unlikeness;
You will see rare beasts, and have unique adventures.

He is the Truth.
Seek Him in the Kingdom of Anxiety;
You will come to a great city that has expected your return
    for years.

He is the Life.
Love Him in the World of the Flesh;
And at your marriage all its occasions shall dance for joy.

THE THIRD SUNDAY OF EPIPHANY

———◀○▶———

'I Am the Way'

Alice Meynell, English, 1847–1922

People are drawn to the revelation of God in Jesus. This poem acknowledges him as the Way whom disciples follow, and their companion in the journey of faith, and the destination to which they come at last.

Thou art the Way
Hadst thou been nothing but the goal
    I cannot say
If thou hadst ever met my soul.

    I cannot see –
I, child of process – if there lies
    An end for me
Full of repose, full of replies.

    I'll not reproach
The road that winds, my feet that err.
    Access, Approach
Art thou, Time, Way, and Wayfarer.

THE FOURTH SUNDAY OF EPIPHANY

Jesus and His Mother

Thom Gunn, Anglo-American, 1929–

In exploring the relationship of Mary with her son (Gospel, Year A*),
Thom Gunn's poem touches on the strangeness of Jesus' identity to those
who were familiar with him (Gospel, Year B) – the ordinary child of
Mary, the carpenter's son, the local boy who has a compelling authority
as teacher and healer, driven by a disturbing obedience which draws him
beyond the conventional and domestic towards itinerant preaching and
painful, separating sacrifice.

My only son, more God's than mine,
Stay in this garden ripe with pears.
The yielding of their substance wears
A modest and contented shine:
And when they weep with age, not brine
But lazy syrup are their tears.
'I am my own and not my own.'

He seemed much like another man,
That silent foreigner who trod
Outside my door with lily rod:
How could I know what I began
Meeting the eyes more furious than
The eyes of Joseph, those of God?
I was my own and not my own.

And who are these twelve labouring men?
I do not understand your words:
I taught you speech, we named the birds,
You marked their big migrations then
Like any child. So turn again
To silence from the place of crowds.
'I am my own and not my own.'

Why are you sullen when I speak?
Here are your tools, the saw and knife
And hammer on your bench. Your life
Is measured here in week and week
Planed as the furniture you make,
And I will teach you like a wife
To be my own and all my own.

Who like an arrogant wind blown
Where he may please, needs no content?
Yet I remember how you went
To speak with scholars in furred gown.
I hear an outcry in the town;
Who carried that dark instrument?
'One all his own and not his own.'

Treading the green and nimble sward
I stare at a strange shadow thrown.
Are you the boy I bore alone,
No doctor near to cut the cord?
I cannot reach to call you Lord,
Answer me as my only son.
'I am my own and not my own.'

The Presentation of Christ in the Temple (Candlemas)

——◄◌►——

Mother and Child (American primitive)
Charles Causley, English, 1917–

The poet offers a Candlemas image of Mary bearing the bright flame of the Christ-child surrounded by the darkness of a fallen creation which he comes to enlighten.

Holding in clear hands
The world's true light
She lifts its perfect flame
Against the night.

About its pulse of fire
Earth and seas run,
Season and moon and star,
The unruly sun.

Upon the hill a scuffed
Thinness of snow,
First of green thorn, a stream
Stopped in its flow.

She keeps within her hand
The careful day
Now the slow wound of night
Has bled away:

Vivid upon her tongue
Unspoken prayers
That she may not outlive
The life she bears.

THE FIFTH SUNDAY OF EPIPHANY
(PROPER 1)

———◄○►———

From *The Color Purple*

Alice Walker, African-American, 1944–

For disciples who seek abundant life, Jesus' command to 'put out into the deep' (Gospel, Year C) is to nurture a contemplative spirit which attends to the vibrant reality of God – who, though incomparable and incomprehensible, is known in the created world (Old Testament and Psalm, Year B), and revealed within themselves and others through the Spirit (New Testament, Year A). The spiritual wisdom of Alice Walker's Shug gives an earthy expression of this contemplative vision; her alert and imaginative faith is a good example of salt which has *not* lost its saltiness (Gospel, Year A).

Here's the thing, say Shug. The thing I believe. God is inside you and inside everybody else. You come into the world with God. But only them that search for it inside find it. And sometimes it just manifest itself even if you not looking, or don't know what you looking for. Trouble do it for most folks, I think. Sorrow, lord. Feeling like shit.

It? I ast.

Yeah, It. God ain't a he or a she, but a It.

But what do it look like? I ast.

Don't look like nothing, she say. It ain't a picture show. It ain't something you can look at apart from anything else, including yourself. I believe God is everything, say Shug. Everything that is or ever was or ever will be. And when you can feel that, and be happy to feel that, you've found It.

Shug a beautiful something, let me tell you. She frown a little, look out cross the yard, lean back in her chair, look like a big rose.

She say, My first step from the old white man was trees. Then air. Then birds. Then other people. But one day when I was sitting quiet and feeling like a motherless child, which I was, it come to me: that feeling of being part of everything, not separate at all. I knew that if I cut a tree, my arm would bleed. And I laughed and I cried and I run all round the house. I knew just what it was. In fact, when it happened you can't miss it. It sort of like you know what, she say, grinning and rubbing high up on my thigh.

Shug ! I say.

Oh, she say. God love all them feelings. That's some of the best stuff God did. And when you know God loves 'em you enjoys 'em a lot more. You can just relax, go with everything that's going, and praise God by liking what you like.

God don't think it dirty? I ast.

Naw, she say. God made it. Listen, God love everything you love – and a mess of stuff you don't. But more than anything else, God love admiration.

You saying God vain, I ast.

Naw, she say. Not vain, just wanting to share a good thing. I think it pisses God off if you walk by the color purple in a field somewhere and don't notice it.

What it do when it pissed off? I ast.

Oh, it make something else. People think pleasing God is all God care about. But any fool living in the world can see it always trying to please us back.

THE SIXTH SUNDAY OF EPIPHANY
(PROPER 2)

————◄◦►————

An African Elegy

Ben Okri, Nigerian, 1959–

In this verse Ben Okri celebrates the inalienable dignity of African people – their joy and enduring hope in suffering are an expression of the spirituality of the Beatitudes (Gospel, Year C). These are the people who 'choose life' even when life's circumstances seem a wilderness (Old Testament, Year A).

> We are the miracles that God made
> To taste the bitter fruit of Time.
> We are precious.
> And one day our suffering
> Will turn into the wonders of the earth.
>
> There are things that burn me now
> Which turn golden when I am happy.
> Do you see the mystery of our pain?
> That we bear poverty
> And are able to sing and dream sweet things
>
> And that we never curse the air when it is warm
> Or the fruit when it tastes so good
> Or the lights that bounce gently on the waters?
> We bless things even in our pain.
> We bless them in silence.

That is why our music is so sweet.
It makes the air remember.
There are secret miracles at work
That only Time will bring forth.
I too have heard the dead singing.

And they tell me that
This life is good
They tell me to live it gently
With fire, and always with hope.
There is wonder here

And there is surprise
In everything the unseen moves.
The ocean is full of songs.
The sky is not an enemy.
Destiny is our friend.

THE SEVENTH SUNDAY OF EPIPHANY (PROPER 3)

────◄○►────

From *Centuries of Meditations*, IV.84

Thomas Traherne, English, 1637–74

The limitless love Jesus teaches his disciples to practise (Gospel, Years A and C) Traherne acknowledges as the love of God dwelling in the human soul.

That God should love in the soul is most easy to believe, because it is most easy to conceive. But it is a greater mystery that the soul should love in itself. If God loveth in the soul, it is the more precious; if the soul loveth, it is the more marvellous. If you ask how a soul that was made of nothing can return so many flames of love, where it should have them or out of what ocean it should communicate them, it is impossible to declare (for it can return those flames upon all eternity, and upon all the creatures and objects in it). Unless we say, as a mirror returneth the very self-same beams it receiveth from the sun, so the soul returneth those beams of love that shine upon it from God. For as a looking-glass is nothing in comparison of the world, yet containeth all the world in it, and seems a fountain of those beams which flow from it, so the soul is nothing in respect of God, yet all eternity is contained within it, and it is the real fountain of that love that proceedeth from it. They are the sunbeams which the glass returneth; yet they flow from the glass and from the sun within it. The mirror is the well-spring of them, because they shine from the sun within the mirror. Which is as deep within the glass as it is high within the heavens. And this showeth the exceeding richness and preciousness of love: it is the love of God shining upon, and dwelling in the soul, for the beams that shine upon it reflect upon others and shine from it.

THE SECOND SUNDAY BEFORE LENT

———◄◦►———

God Speaks

Charles Péguy, French, 1873–1914,
translated by Ann and Julian Green

Jesus teaches that his disciples should not be anxious (Gospel, Year A), and he embodies calm trust as he sleeps in the boat and wakes to still both the storm and the disciples' fear (Gospel, Year C*). Here Péguy writes of sleep as beatitude.

I don't like the man who doesn't sleep, says God.
Sleep is the friend of man.
Sleep is the friend of God.
Sleep is perhaps the most beautiful thing I have created.
And I myself rested on the seventh day.
He whose heart is pure, sleeps. And he who sleeps has a pure
　　heart.
That is the great secret of being as indefatigable as a child.
Of having that strength in the legs that a child has.
Those new legs, those new souls,
And to begin afresh every morning, ever new,
Like young hope, new hope…
He who doesn't sleep is unfaithful to Hope.
And it is the great infidelity.
Because it is infidelity to the greatest Faith.
Poor children, they conduct their business with wisdom during
　　the day.
But when evening comes, they can't make up their minds,
They can't be resigned to trust my wisdom for the space of one
　　night
With the conduct and the governing of their business.

As if I wasn't capable, if you please, of looking after it a little.
Of watching over it.
Of governing and conducting, and all that kind of stuff.
I have a great deal more business to look after, poor people,
    I govern creation, maybe that is more difficult.
You might perhaps, and no harm done, leave your business in
    my hands, O wise men.
Maybe I am just as wise as you are.
You might perhaps leave it for me for the space of a night.
While you are asleep
At last
And the next morning you might find it not too badly damaged
    perhaps...
Put off until tomorrow those tears which fill your eyes and your
    head,
Flooding you, rolling down your cheeks, those tears which
    stream down your cheeks.
Because between now and tomorrow, maybe I, God, will have
    passed by your way.
Human wisdom says: Woe to the man who puts off what he has
    to do until tomorrow.
And I say Blessed, blessed is the man who puts off what he has to
    do until tomorrow.
Blessed is he who puts off. That is to say Blessed is he who
    hopes. And who sleeps.

The Sunday Next Before Lent

The Incarnation, and Passion

Henry Vaughan, Anglo-Welsh, 1622–95

The Gospel readings for Years A*, B* and C* offer the story of the
Transfiguration of Christ as the year turns towards the season of focus
upon his suffering and death. This poem celebrates Christ's laying aside
his glory for the sake of his rebellious creation.

> Lord! when thou didst thy self undress
> Laying by thy robes of glory,
> To make us more, thou wouldst be less,
> And becamest a woeful story.
>
> To put on clouds instead of light,
> And clothe the morning-star with dust,
> Was a translation of such height
> As, but in thee, was ne'r expressed;
>
> Brave worms, and Earth! that thus could have
> A God enclosed within your Cell,
> Your maker pent up in a grave,
> Life locked in death, heaven in a shell;
>
> Ah, my dear Lord! what couldst thou spy
> In this impure, rebellious clay,
> That made thee thus resolve to die
> For those that kill thee every day?
>
> O what strange wonders could thee move
> To slight thy precious blood, and breath!
> Sure it was *Love*, my Lord; for *Love*
> Is only stronger far than death.

ASH WEDNESDAY

—◄◊►—

From *The Whale,* part of the *Physiologus*

Translated from Anglo-Saxon by Professor Charles W. Kennedy

In this excerpt from the ancient bestiary the faithful are warned of the
deceitfulness and alluring vanity of evil. Milton employed the same
imagery in Book One of *Paradise Lost* (lines 192–210).

Now I will fashion   the tale of a fish,
With wise wit singing   in measured strains
The song of the Great Whale.   Often unwittingly
Ocean-mariners   meet with this monster,
Fastitocalon,   fierce and menacing,
The Great Sea-Swimmer   of the ocean-streams.
Like a rough rock   is the Whale's appearance,
Or as if there were swaying   by the shore of the sea
A great mass of sedge   in the midst of the sand dunes;
So it seems to sailors   they see an island,
And they firmly fasten   their high-prowed ships
With anchor-ropes   to the land that is no land,
Hobble their sea-steeds   at ocean's end,
Land bold on the island   and leave their barks
Moored at the water's edge   in the wave's embrace.
There they encamp,   the sea-weary sailors,
Fearing no danger.   They kindle a fire;
High on the island   the hot flames blaze
And joy returns   to travel-worn hearts
Eager for rest.   Then, crafty in evil,
When the whale feels the sailors   are fully set
Are firmly lodged,   enjoying fair weather,
Suddenly with his prey   Ocean's Guest plunges
Down in the salt wave   seeking the depths,

In the hall of death   drowning the sailors and ships.
   Such is the manner of demons,   the devils' way,
Luring from virtue,   inciting to lust,
By secret power   deceiving men's souls
That they may seek help   at the hands of their foes
And, fixed in sin,   find abode with the Fiend...
   A second trait has he,   the proud Sea-Thrasher,
Even more marvellous: when hunger torments
And the fierce Water-Monster   is fain of food,
Then the Ocean-Warden   opens his mouth,
Unlocks his wide jaws,   and a winsome odour
Comes from his belly;   other kinds of fish
Are deceived thereby,   all eagerly swimming
To where the sweet fragrance   comes flowing forth.
In unwary schools   they enter within
Till the wide mouth is filled.   Then swiftly the Whale
Over his sea-prey   snaps his grim jaws.
   So it is with him   in this transient time
Who takes heed to his life   too late and too little,
Letting vain delights   through their luring fragrance
Ensnare his soul...

fastitocalon – literally 'tortoise shield', describing a large
whale.

THE FIRST SUNDAY OF LENT

If You Seek . . . song

Thomas Merton, American, 1915–68

As the Gospel readings direct us towards Jesus' time alone in the wilderness, a poem on solitude.

If you seek a heavenly light
I, Solitude, am your professor!

I go before you into emptiness,
Raise strange suns for your new mornings,
Opening the windows
Of your innermost apartment.

When I, loneliness, give my special signal
Follow my silence, follow where I beckon!
Fear not, little beast, little spirit
(Thou word and animal)
I, Solitude, am angel
And have prayed in your name.

Look at the empty, wealthy night
The pilgrim moon!
I am the appointed hour,
The "now" that cuts
Time like a blade.

I am the unexpected flash
Beyond "yes," beyond "no,"
The forerunner of the Word of God.

Follow my ways and I will lead you
To golden-haired suns,
Logos and music, blameless joys,
Innocent of questions
And beyond answers:
For I, Solitude, am thine own self:
I, Nothingness, am thy All.
I, Silence, am thy Amen!

THE SECOND SUNDAY OF LENT

I Am the Great Sun
(from a Normandy crucifix of 1632)
Charles Causley, English, 1917–

The RCL Gospel readings give the story of the Transfiguration today, whereas the Gospel readings for Years A*, B* and C* present Jesus as the one who is destined to suffer. In Causley's compelling lyric, the images for Jesus are glorious and worthy of love and obedience – but he is unrecognized and rejected.

> I am the great sun, but you do not see me,
>> I am your husband, but you turn away.
> I am the captive, but you do not free me,
>> I am the captain you will not obey.
>
> I am the truth, but you will not believe me,
>> I am the city where you will not stay,
> I am your wife, your child, but you will leave me,
>> I am the God to whom you will not pray.
>
> I am your counsel, but you do not hear me,
>> I am the lover whom you will betray.
> I am the victor, but you do not cheer me,
>> I am the holy dove whom you will slay.
>
> I am your life, but if you will not name me,
> Seal up your soul with tears and never blame me.

THE THIRD SUNDAY OF LENT

Discipline

George Herbert, Anglo-Welsh, 1593–1633

In this poem on repentance, as he confesses his failures, Herbert calls on
God to be true to his own divine nature and to let his love supersede his
anger.

Throw away thy rod,
Throw away thy wrath;
O my God,
Take the gentle path.

For my heart's desire
Unto thine is bent;
I aspire
To a full consent.

Not a word or look
I affect to own,
But by book,
And thy book alone.

Though I fail, I weep;
Though I halt in pace,
Yet I creep
To the throne of grace.

Then let wrath remove,
Love will do the deed;
For with love
Stonie hearts will bleed.

Love is swift of foot;
Love's a man of warre,
    And can shoot,
And can hit from farre.

Who can 'scape his bow?
That which wrought on thee,
    Brought thee low,
Needs must work on me.

Throw away thy rod:
Though man frailties hath,
    Thou art God;
Throw away thy wrath.

THE FOURTH SUNDAY OF LENT

To Keep a True Lent

Robert Herrick, English, 1591–1674

For 'Refreshment Sunday' a reminder of the nature of true religion.

Is this a Fast, to keep
    The Larder leane?
      And cleane
From fat of Veales, and Sheep?

Is it to quit the dish
    Of Flesh, yet still
      To fill
The platter high with Fish?

Is it to fast an houre,
    Or rag'd to go,
      Or show
A down-cast look, and sowre?

No: 'tis a Fast, to dole
    Thy sheaf of wheat,
      And meat,
Unto the hungry Soule.

It is to fast from strife,
    From old debate,
      And hate;
To circumcise thy life.

To shew a heart grief-rent;
   To sterve thy sin,
     Not bin;
And that's to keep thy Lent.

MOTHERING SUNDAY

————◄◉►————

Woman to Child

Judith Wright, Australian, 1915–2000

In this poem a mother reflects on the inseparable connection between herself and the child who grew within her body – the physical generation of life and love, and the physical generation of death and sin.

You who were darkness warmed my flesh
where out of darkness rose the seed.
Then all a world I made in me;
all the world you hear and see
hung upon my dreaming blood.

There moved the multitudinous stars,
and coloured birds and fishes moved.
There swam the sliding continents.
All time lay rolled in me, and sense,
and love that knew not its beloved.

O node and focus of the world;
I hold you deep within that well
you shall escape and not escape –
that mirrors still your sleeping shape;
that nurtures still your crescent cell.

I wither and you break from me;
yet though you dance in living light
I am the earth, I am the root,
I am the stem that fed the fruit,
the link that joins you to the night.

THE FIFTH SUNDAY OF LENT
(PASSIONTIDE BEGINS)

———◄○►———

The Grave

Translated from Anglo-Saxon by Henry Wadsworth Longfellow,
American, 1807–82

This grim poem tells of the grave where all mortal beings will surely find
their end. Jesus raises Lazarus from the foul tomb (Gospel, Year A), a
tomb which – in love and obedience – will become his own resting place
(Gospel, Years B and C), thereby transforming a place of terror into a bed
of hope for his people.

> For thee was a house built
> Ere thou wast born,
> For thee was a mould meant
> Ere thou of mother camest.
> But it is not made ready,
> Nor its depth measured,
> Nor is it seen
> How long it shall be.
> Now I bring thee
> Where thou shalt be;
> Now I shall measure thee,
> And the mould afterwards.
>
> Thy house is not
> Highly timbered,
> It is unhigh and low;
> When thou art therein,
> The heel-ways are low,
> The side-ways unhigh.
> The roof is built

Thy breast full nigh,
So thou shalt in mould
Dwell full cold,
Dimly and dark.

Doorless is that house,
And dark it is within;
There thou art fast detained,
And Death hath the key.
Loathsome is that earth-house,
And grim within to dwell,
And worms shall divide thee.

Thus thou art laid,
And leavest thy friends;
Thou hast no friend
Who will come to thee,
Who will ever see
How that house pleaseth thee,
Who will ever open
The door for thee,
And descend after thee,
For soon thou art loathsome
And hateful to see.

PALM SUNDAY
(LITURGY OF THE PASSION)

---◄○►---

Two poems for the beginning of Holy Week: first a meditation on the donkey which carries Jesus into Jerusalem, and then a poem of prayer at the outset of our own journey to the Cross.

Upon the Ass that Bore Our Saviour
Richard Crashaw, English, 1612–49

Hath only Anger an Omnipotence
    In Eloquence?
Within the lips of Love and Joy doth dwell
    No miracle?
Why else had Baalam's Ass a tongue to chide
    His Master's pride?
And thou (Heaven-burthen'd Beast) hast ne'er a word
    To praise thy Lord?
That he should find a Tongue and vocal Thunder
    Was a great wonder.
But o methinks 'tis a far greater one
    That thou find'st none.

Prayer for Holy Week

Elizabeth Jennings, English, 1926–

Love me in my willingness to suffer
Love me in the gifts I wish to offer
    Teach me how you love and have to die
      And I will try

Somehow to forget myself and give
Life and joy so dead things start to live.
    Let me show now an untrammelled joy,
      Gold without alloy.

You know I have no cross but want to learn,
How to change and to the poor would turn.
    I can almost worship stars and moon
      And the sun at noon

But when I'm low I only beg you to
Ask me anything, I'll try to do
    What you need. I trust your energy.
      Share it then with me.

MONDAY IN HOLY WEEK

————◀◦▶————

Hymn

Alexander Pope, English, 1688–1744

Pope's contemplation of Christ's sufferings calls forth love within him as a response.

Thou art my God, sole object of my love;
Not for hope of endless joys above;
Not for the fear of endless pains below,
Which they who love thee must not undergo.
For me, and such as me, thou deignst to bear
An ignominious cross, the nails, the spear:
A thorny crown transpierced thy sacred brow,
While bloody sweats from every member flow.
For me in tortures thou resignst thy breath,
Embraced me on the cross, and saved me by death.
And can these sufferings fail my heart to move?
Such as then was, and is, thy love to me,
Such is, and shall be still, my love to thee –
To thee, Redeemer! mercy's sacred spring!
My God, my Father, Maker, and my King!

TUESDAY IN HOLY WEEK

————◄○►————

Phoenix

D. H. Lawrence, English, 1885–1930

Lawrence's poem is typical: a fierce challenge to seize the fullness of life
and to accept loss and sacrifice as the way of rebirth. For the followers of
Christ, this is the Paschal journey into Easter immortality (Gospel, Years
A, B and C).

Are you willing to be sponged out, erased, cancelled,
made nothing?
Are you willing to be made nothing?
dipped into oblivion?

If not, you will never really change.

The phoenix renews her youth
only when she is burnt, burnt alive, burnt down
to hot and flocculent ash.
Then the small stirring of a new small bub in the nest
with strands of down like floating ash
Shows that she is renewing her youth like the eagle,
immortal bird.

WEDNESDAY IN HOLY WEEK

——◄◦►——

The Job, from The Book of Judas, 5
Brendan Kennelly, Irish, 1936–

Kennelly's epic poem *The Book of Judas* gives the betrayer many voices as it explores the cultural and theological phenomena surrounding one man who is hated and reviled through history. Here Judas has the voice of an embittered idealist who has been wrongfully overlooked.

Why didn't I get the job? The thought
Is something of an obsession.
If I'd been appointed I'd have changed
The image of the Apostolic Succession.

With my special talent who knows
What might have happened?
Would the church be facing
Its present state of spiritual collapse?

Peter was first choice.
Judas the traitor, Peter the rock:
Perish the labels; we soldiered together once.
Peter was able-bodied, quick-tempered, strong-voiced,
Good-hearted. But did he do the trick?
Or is the rock self-smashed into smithereens?
Why do the most living hearts
Attract the deadest has-beens?
How did that passionate adventure
Become a bad theological lecture?
How did the agony of loving eyes
Become a sordid political enterprise?
Although my soul is helplessly adrift

I have a few questions left.
There'll be no answers till the polished men
Get the smell of blood from the hill again.

MAUNDY THURSDAY

———◄o►———

As the readings and liturgy today bring into special focus the servanthood of Jesus, expressed in his foot-washing, and the institution of the Eucharist, so Lawrence's poem on the beauty of touch, and Dix's unsurpassed prose acclaiming the Eucharist.

Future Religion
D. H. Lawrence, English, 1885–1930

The future of religion is in the mystery of touch.
The mind is touchless, so is the will, so is the spirit.
First comes the death, then the pure aloneness, which is
    permanent
then the resurrection into touch.

From *The Shape of the Liturgy*

Dom Gregory Dix, English, 1901–52

Was ever another command so obeyed? For century after century, spreading slowly to every continent and country and among every race on earth, this action has been done, in every conceivable human circumstance, from every conceivable human need from infancy and before it to extreme old age and after it, from the pinnacles of earthly greatness to the refuge of the fugitives in the caves and dens of the earth. Men have found no better thing than this to do for kings at their crowning and for criminals going to the scaffold; for armies in triumph or for a bride and bridegroom in a little country church; for the proclamation of a dogma or for a good crop of wheat; for the wisdom of the Parliament of a mighty nation or for a sick old woman afraid to die; for a schoolboy sitting an examination or for Columbus setting out to discover America; for the famine of whole provinces or for the soul of a dead lover; in thankfulness because my father did not die of pneumonia; for a village headman much tempted to return to fetich because the yams had failed; because the Turk was at the gates of Vienna; for the repentance of Margaret; for the settlement of a strike; for a son for a barren woman; for Captain so-and-so, wounded and prisoner of war; while the lions roared in the nearby amphitheatre; on the beach at Dunkirk; while the hiss of scythes in the thick June grass came faintly through the windows of the church; tremulously, by an old monk on the fiftieth anniversary of his vows; furtively, by an exiled bishop who had hewn timber all day in a prison camp near Murmansk; gorgeously, for the canonisation of S. Joan of Arc – one could fill many pages with the reasons why men have done this, and not tell a hundredth part of them. And best of all, week by week and month by month, on a hundred thousand successive Sundays, faithfully, unfailingly, across all the parishes of Christendom, the pastors have done this just to *make* the *plebs sancta Dei* – the holy common people of God.

GOOD FRIDAY

—◁◦▷—

The Tree of Calvary is a venerable subject in British poetry. In Bowen's poem, translated from Welsh, the native rowan tree, with its red berries, becomes an evocative symbol of Christ's passion.

The medieval lyric which follows celebrates the victory of love which is won on the Cross.

The Rowan Tree

Euros Bowen, Welsh, 1904–88, translated by Oliver Davies

You can see it above the river's hollow bank, on the edge,
    of gorse and wind,
A crack in the bareness of rock is its earth.

The twisted form of its grey trunk stands,
    gaunt and bare,
Shaped like a wooden cross.

Its branches are arms outstretched, darkened
    by a wound in the chest,
Rough and harsh as the ribs of Christ.

And blood trickles on this tree, on the edge
    of gorse and wind,
Blood which breaks from the swell of God's pity.

Christ's Love-Song

Anonymous, Middle English

Love me brought,
And love me wrought,
    Man, to be thy fere.
Love me fed,
And love me led
    And love me lettet here.

Love me slew,
And love me drew,
    And love me laid on bier.
Love is my piece;
For love I chese,
    Man to buyen dear.

Ne dread thee nought,
I have thee sought,
    Bothen day and night,
To haven thee
Well is me,
    I haven thee won in fight.

fere – mate; *lettet* – kept; *chese* – chose.

EASTER EVE

W. H. Vanstone's poem on the entombment and resurrection of Christ comes in his final book, *Fare Well in Christ*, a Christian meditation on death. The writer and critic George Steiner reflects on the nature of Holy Saturday – of waiting between suffering and hope.

Joseph of Arimathea's Easter, from *Fare Well in Christ*
W. H. Vanstone, English, 1923–99

'He's gone,' says Joseph, and, with Pilate's leave
Eases the nails and lowers him from the Tree,
Wraps him in reverent and tender thoughts
And lays him in the cave called Memory.

That cave is deeply hewn in Joseph's heart:
All that's within will always be his own:
In memory's cave the treasure of his past
Is safe for ever, walled and sealed by stone.

'He's safe,' says Joseph, 'safe in this cool place
And no one now can take my Lord away.
In years to come I'll still see his dear face
As clearly as I've seen it on this day.'

'He's gone!' cries Joseph at the empty tomb:
But Mary says, 'He's left a word for you:
He cannot rest content to be your past,
So he has risen to be your future too.'

From *Real Presences*, III.7

George Steiner, American, 1929–

There is one particular day in Western history about which neither historical record nor myth nor Scripture make report. It is a Saturday. And it has become the longest of days. We know of that Good Friday which Christianity holds to have been that of the Cross. But the non-Christian, the atheist, knows of it as well. This is to say that he knows of the injustice, of the interminable suffering, of the waste, of the brute enigma of ending, which so largely make up not only the historical dimension of the human condition, but the everyday fabric of our personal lives. We know, ineluctably, of the pain, of the failure of love, of the solitude which are our history and private fate. We know also about Sunday. To the Christian, that day signifies an intimation, both assured and precarious, both evident and beyond comprehension, of resurrection, of a justice and a love that have conquered death. If we are non-Christians or non-believers, we know of that Sunday in precisely analogous terms. We conceive of it as the day of liberation from inhumanity and servitude. We look to resolutions, be they therapeutic or political, be they social or messianic. The lineaments of that Sunday carry the name of hope (there is no word less deconstructible).

But ours is the long day's journey of the Saturday. Between suffering, aloneness, unutterable waste on the one hand and the dream of liberation, of rebirth on the other. In the face of the torture of a child, of the death of love which is Friday, even the greatest art and poetry are helpless. In the Utopia of the Sunday, the aesthetic will, presumably, no longer have logic or necessity. The apprehensions and figurations in the play of the metaphysical imagining, in the poem and the music, which tell of pain and of hope, of the flesh which is said to taste of ash and of the spirit which is said to have the savour of fire, are always Sabbatarian. They have risen out of an immensity of waiting which is that of man. Without them, how could we be patient?

EASTER DAY

———◄○►———

The women find the tomb empty and the body they have come to anoint is gone. Clampitt's lines on Easter morning express the grace of this resurrection emptiness after all the garrulous violence of trial and crucifixion. In the Gospel readings for Years A★, B★ and C★, Mary Magdalene sees the risen Lord – an ecstatic encounter which Ann Griffiths imagines in the second poem.

Easter Morning, from *Triptych*
Amy Clampitt, American, 1920–94

a stone at dawn
cold water in the basin
these walls' rough plaster
imageless
after the hammering
of so much insistence
on the need for naming
after the travesties
that passed as faces,
grace: the unction
of sheer nonexistence
upwelling in this
hyacinthine freshet
of the unnamed
the faceless

I Saw Him Standing

Ann Griffiths, Welsh, 1776–1805, translated by Rowan Williams

Under the dark trees, there he stands,
there he stands; shall he not draw my eyes?
I thought I knew a little
how he compels, beyond all things, but now
he stands there in the shadows. It will be
Oh, such a daybreak, such bright morning,
when I shall wake to see him
as he is.

He is called Rose of Sharon, for his skin
is clear, his skin is flushed with blood,
his body lovely and exact; how he compels
beyond ten thousand rivals. There he stands,
my friend, the friend of guilt and helplessness,
to steer my hollow body
over the sea.

The earth is full of masks and fetishes,
what is there here for me? are these like him?
Keep company with him and you will know:
no kin, no likeness to those empty eyes.
He is a stranger to them all, great Jesus.
What is there here for me? I know
what I have longed for. Him to hold
me always.

THE SECOND SUNDAY OF EASTER

———◄◦►———

From *Invisible Man*

Ralph Ellison, African-American, 1914–94

In the Prologue to Ellison's powerful novel about one black man's experience of racism in the United States, his hero says: 'I am an invisible man . . . I am a man of substance, of flesh and bone, fibre and liquids – and I might even be said to possess a mind. I am invisible, understand, simply because people refuse to see me.' In this excerpt from the final chapters, the hero accepts that all the hurts and wounds of prejudice have become an integral part of his unique identity: he is to be seen and known by his scars, as Christ is known to Thomas (Gospel, Years A, B and C).

And now all past humiliations became precious parts of my experience, and for the first time, leaning against that stone wall in the sweltering night, I began to accept my past and, as I accepted it, I felt memories welling up within me. It was as though I'd learned suddenly to look around corners; images of past humiliations flickered through my head and I saw that they were more than separate experiences. They were me; they defined me. I was my experiences and my experiences were me, and no blind men, no matter how powerful they became, even if they conquered the world, could take that, or change one single itch, taunt, laugh, cry, scar, ache, rage or pain of it.

Easter 1984

Les Murray, Australian, 1938–

Murray contemplates Easter with the themes of Orwell's novel *Nineteen
Eighty-Four* in mind, which was written in 1948 as a study of totalitarian-
ism and cynical manipulation of notions of political and personal 'freedom'.

When we saw human dignity
healing humans in the middle of the day

we moved in on him slowly
under the incalculable gravity

of old freedom, of our own freedom,
under atmospheres of consequence, of justice

under which no one needs to thank anyone.
If this was God, we would get even.

And in the end we nailed him,
lashed, spittled, stretched him limb from limb

We would settle with dignity
for the anguish it had caused us,

we'd send it to be abstract again,
we would set it free.

O

But we had raised up evolution.
It would not stop being human.

Ever afterwards, the accumulation
of freedom would end in this man

whipped, bloodied, getting the treatment.
It would look like man himself getting it.

He was freeing us, painfully, of freedom,
justice, dignity – he was discharging them

of their deadly ambiguous deposit,
remaking out of them the primal day

in which he was free not to have borne it
and we were free not to have done it,

free never to torture man again,
free to believe him risen.

O

Remember the day when life increased,
explainably or outright, was haloed in poignancy,

straight life, given not attained, unlurching ecstasy,
arrest of the guards for once, and ourself released,

splendour taking detail, beyond the laughter-and-tears
if those were a gateway to it, a still or moving utterness

in and all around us. Four have been this human
night and day, steadily. Three fell, two went on.

A laser of this would stand the litter-bound or Lazarus
upright, stammering, or unshroud absent Jesus
whose anguish was to be for a whole day lost to this,
making of himself the companionway of our species

up from where such love is an unreal, half-forgotten
peak, and not the baseline of the human.

THE THIRD SUNDAY OF EASTER

———◄○►———

In these two poems Dickinson celebrates the abiding presence of the risen Saviour.

Unto me?

Emily Dickinson, American, 1830–86

"Unto Me?" I do not know you –
Where may be your House?

"I am Jesus – Late of Judea –
Now – of Paradise" –

Wagons – have you – to convey me?
This is far from Thence –

"Arms of Mine – sufficient Phaeton –
Trust Omnipotence" –

I am spotted – "I am Pardon" –
I am small – "The Least
Is esteemed in Heaven the Chiefest –
Occupy my House" –

Phaeton – a type of carriage.

The Blunder is to Estimate

Emily Dickinson, American, 1830–86

The blunder is to estimate, –
"Eternity is *Then*,"
We say, as of a station.
Meanwhile he is so near,
He joins me in my ramble,
Divides abode with me,
No friend have I that so persists
As this Eternity.

THE FOURTH SUNDAY OF EASTER

―――◄◦►―――

The Passionate Shepherd to His Love
Christopher Marlowe, English, 1564–93

Today's focus on Christ the Shepherd allows Marlowe's pastoral love poem to be read as a kind of English Song of Songs, in which Christ the Shepherd woos the beloved soul in whom he delights.

> Come live with me and be my Love,
> And we will all the pleasures prove
> That hills and valleys, dales and fields,
> Or woods or steepy mountain yields.
>
> And we will sit upon the rocks,
> And see the shepherds feed their flocks
> By shallow rivers, to whose falls
> Melodious birds sing madrigals.
>
> And I will make thee beds of roses
> And a thousand fragrant posies;
> A cap of flowers, and a kirtle
> Embroider'd all with leaves of myrtle.
>
> A gown made of the finest wool
> Which from our pretty lambs we pull;
> Fair-lined slippers for the cold,
> With buckles of the purest gold.
>
> A belt of straw and ivy-buds
> With coral clasps and amber studs:
> And if these pleasures may thee move,
> Come live with me and be my Love.

The shepherd swains shall dance and sing
For thy delight each May morning:
If these delights thy mind may move,
Then live with me and be my Love.

kirtle – a coat or skirt; *swains* – young men, lovers.

THE FIFTH SUNDAY OF EASTER

Easter Day

Edmund Spenser, English, 1552–99

Spenser's sonnet urges us to imitate the dying and rising Christ in love of
God and neighbour.

Most glorious Lord of life, that on this day,
    Didst make Thy triumph over death and sin:
    And having harrow'd hell, didst bring away
    Captivity thence captive, us to win:
This joyous day, dear Lord, with joy begin,
    And grant that we for whom Thou diddest die
    Being with Thy dear blood clean wash'd from sin,
    May live for ever in felicity.
And that Thy love we weighing worthily,
    May likewise love Thee for the same again:
    And for Thy sake that all like dear didst buy,
    With love may one another entertain.
So let us love, dear love, like as we ought,
    Love is the lesson which the Lord us taught.

THE SIXTH SUNDAY OF EASTER

―――◀◦▶―――

Song of the Soul that Rejoices in Knowing God Through Faith

St John of the Cross, 1542–91, translated from the Spanish by
Seamus Heaney, Irish, 1939–

Through the death and resurrection of Christ the Spirit of Truth flows to
the faithful. These mystical verses, incorporated into Part XI of Heaney's
poem *Station Island*, celebrate the life of God which floods the world –
invisible, uncontainable, yet sacramentally present, the source of life and
healing for all.

> How well I know that fountain, filling, running,
> although it is the night.
>
> That eternal fountain, hidden away,
> I know its haven and its secrecy
> although it is the night.
>
> But not its source because it does not have one,
> which is all sources' source and origin
> although it is the night.
>
> No other thing can be so beautiful.
> Here the earth and heaven drink their fill
> although it is the night.
>
> I know no sounding-line can find its bottom,
> nobody ford or plumb its deepest fathom
> although it is the night.

And the current that is generated there,
as far as it wills to, it can flow that far
    although it is the night.

And from these two a third current proceeds
which neither of these two, I know, precedes
    although it is the night.

This eternal fountain hides and splashes
within this living bread that is life to us
    although it is the night.

Hear it calling out to every creature.
And they drink these waters, although it is dark here
    because it is the night.

I am repining for this living fountain.
Within this bread of life I see it plain
    although it is the night.

ASCENSION DAY

Ascension Thursday

Saunders Lewis, Welsh, 1893–1985, translated by Oliver Davies

Lewis celebrates the mystery of the Ascension in the sacramental beauty of the dawning day, where all things created worship their Maker and Saviour.

What is happening this May morning on the hillside?
See there, the gold of the broom and the laburnum
And the bright surplice of the thorn's shoulder
And the intent emerald of the grass and the still calves;

See the candelabra of the chestnut tree alight
The bushes kneel and the mute beech, like a nun,
The cuckoo's two notes above the bright hush of the stream,
And the form of the mist that curls from the censer of the
  meadows.

Come out, you men, from the council houses
Before the rabbits run, come with the weasel to see
The elevation of the unblemished host from the earth,
The Father kiss the Son in the white dew.

The Seventh Sunday of Easter
(Sunday after Ascension Day)

———◀◦▶———

From *Ascension*

Cynewulf, Anglo-Saxon, late-eighth century, translated by
Professor Charles Kennedy (1952)

Drawing on a homily of Pope Gregory the Great, the poet urges the
faithful to leap upwards like the ascending Christ, reaching forwards in
faith and good works so as to continually dwell with him and his saints.

>   Yet by grace of the Spirit
> A glory has come   for the thanes of God
> Since the Ascension   of the Eternal Son!
>   Of Him sang Solomon,   son of David
> Versed in songs   and spiritual grace,
> The Ruler of nations,   pronouncing this word:
>   "It is widely known   that the King shall come,
> The Lord of might,   leaping upon the mountains,
> Skipping upon the hills,   and girding with glory
> The knolls and high dunes;   He shall redeem the world,
> All who live on earth,   by that noble leaping."
>   It was the first leap   when our Lord descended
> To the spotless Virgin,   and free from sin
> Took human flesh.   That came for a comfort
> To all the dwellers   over all the earth.
> It was the second leap   when the Babe was born
> Cradled in a manger   in swaddling clothes,
> The glory of all glories   in the guise of a child.
> It was the third leap   when the Lord of heaven,
> The Father, the Comforter,   mounted the Cross.
> It was the fourth leap   when He left the Tree
> And turned to the sepulchre,   fast in the tomb.

It was the fifth leap   when He harrowed hell
With bitter torment   and bound her king,
The fiends' fierce Spokesman,   with bands of fire
Where he still lies fettered,   fast in his sin.
It was the sixth leap   when our Lord in triumph
Ascended on high   to His former home.
In that holy hour   the angel host
Grew blithe with rapture   and blissful joy
Beholding the Lord of glory,   the Leader of princes,
Returning to His native country,   those shining courts.
Then for the citizens of heaven,   for all the saints,
Came eternal joy   from the triumph of their Prince.
    As here on earth's soil   God's Son Eternal
Mounted by leaps   above the high hills,
Bold on the mountains,   so we mortal men
In our hearts' musings   must mount by leaps
From strength to strength,   and strive for glory,
That we may ascend   by holy works
To the highest heavens,   where are joy and hope,
A goodly band of thanes.   Great is our need
In our secret souls   that we seek salvation,
If we have in our hearts   a fervent faith
That the Healing Son,   the Living Saviour,
With our own body   ascended from earth.

Day of Pentecost
(Whit Sunday)

———◄○►———

In these three poems the Spirit-dove descends as bird of cleansing fiery love, as generous distributor of gifts, as exuberant giver of life and inspiration of praise.

From *Little Gidding,* the final section of *Four Quartets*

T. S. Eliot, Anglo-American, 1888–1965

The dove descending breaks the air
With flame of incandescent terror
Of which the tongues declare
The one discharge from sin and error.
The only hope, or else despair
    Lies in the choice of pyre or pyre –
    To be redeemed from fire by fire.

Who then devised the torment? Love.
Love is the unfamiliar Name
Behind the hands that wove
The intolerable shirt of flame
Which human power cannot remove.
    We only live, only suspire
    Consumed by either fire or fire.

The Dove, from the *Physiologus*

Anglo-Saxon, translated by Jessie L. Weston (1913)

With the dove we good customs find
That by us should be borne in mind,
Seven qualities good hath she
Which may well our ensample be.
The Dove hath in her no gall;
Be we simple and soft withal.
Nor her living as thief dost win;
Hold we robbery for a sin.
She lives not on worms but on seed;
On Christ's lore we should feed.
To other birds is she a mother;
So ought we to be to each other.
As a moan and a groan her song;
So we should confess our wrong.
She in water the hawk doth see;
Warned in book of the fiend are we.
In the rock doth she make her nest;
In Christ's mercy our hope should rest.

To the Holy Spirit

James McAuley, Australian, 1917–76

Leaving your fragrant rest on the summit of morning calm,
Descend, Bird of Paradise, from the high mountain;
And, plumed with glowing iris along each curving wire,
Visit in time our regions of eucalypt and palm.

Dance, prophetic bird, in rippling spectrums of fire,
Ray forth your incandescent ritual like a fountain;
Let your drab earthly mate that watches in morning calm
Unseen, be filled with the nuptial splendours of your
    desire.

Engender upon our souls your sacred rhythm: inspire
The trembling breath of the flute, the exultant cosmic
    psalm,
The dance that breaks into flower beneath the storm-
    voiced mountain;
Array in your dazzling intricate plumage the swaying choir.

TRINITY SUNDAY

———◄○►———

Trinitie Sunday, from *The Temple*
George Herbert, Anglo-Welsh, 1593–1633

In the threefold patterns of this poem the solitary human voice appeals to the triune Lord – Creator, Saviour, Sanctifier – to redeem the past, present and future and to enrich fallible human thoughts, words and deeds with the virtues tending towards divine Life, which is our source and sustenance and eternal satisfaction.

> Lord, who hast form'd me out of mud,
>> And hast redeem'd me through thy bloud,
>> And sanctifi'd me to do good,
>
> Purge all my sinnes done heretofore;
>> For I confesse my heavie score,
>> And I will strive to sinne no more.
>
> Enrich my heart, mouth, hands in me,
>> With faith, with hope, with charitie,
>> That I may runne, rise, rest with thee.

Day of Thanksgiving for Holy Communion (Corpus Christi)

――◄○►――

At the Eucharist

G. A. Studdert Kennedy, Anglo-Irish, 1883–1929

This meditation on the Eucharist, written during the horrors of the First
World War by the much loved chaplain 'Woodbine Willie', celebrates the
sacramentality of all life created, redeemed and sustained by the
'omnipresent Love' of God in Christ.

> How through this Sacrament of simple things
> The great God burns His way,
> I know not – He is there.
> The silent air
> Is pulsing with the presence of His grace,
> Almost I feel a face
> Bend o'er me as I kneel,
> While on my ears there steal
> The strains of 'Agnus Dei' softly sung.
> How it calls – calls Heaven to earth,
> Calls Christ to birth,
> And pleads for man's Redemption
> With his God.
> Here star and sod
> Unite to sing their Maker's praise,
> While through the windows, broken rays
> Of crimson sunlight make a path
> For Him to tread.
> Just common bread?
> The artist's colour blazing bright,
> The subtle scheme of shade and light,

That thrills our souls to ecstasy,
Is bread.
The notes that wed,
And weave a wonderland of sound,
Wherein our hearts may wander round,
And reach the heart of God's red rose,
Where beauty dwells alone and grows
Sublime in solitude,
All these are bread.
Are they not born of earth and rain
Becoming tissue of man's brain,
The vehicle of every thought?
The Spirit that our God bestows,
The mystery that loves and knows,
The very soul our Saviour bought
Speaks through a body born of bread –
And wine.
The clinging vine
That climbs some crumbled wall in France,
Drinks in the Love of God,
His precious Blood,
Poured out in beams that dance
Through long-drawn summer days,
Swift golden rays of sunshine,
That are stored within the grape
Until it swells
And spills their splendour
Into wine
To fill the chalice of the Lord
Then earth and heaven intertwine;
The Word
Takes flesh and dwells with men,
And once again
Dim eyes may see
His gentle glory shine,

The glory of humility,
Which in creation stoops to raise,
Through time's eternity of days,
Our weakness to His strength,
For neither length,
Nor breadth nor depth nor height,
Stays now the piercing of that light
Of omnipresent Love,
It runs red fire through our veins,
The Life divine,
In common wine,
Thrills through the matter of our brains,
Begetting dreams,
And gleams
Of God – swift golden speech,
And charity that burns to reach
The very depths of hell,
And lift them up to Christ,
Who has our thirsty souls sufficed,
Till they are drunk with God.

PROPER 4

———◄◦►———

The Say-but-the-word Centurion Attempts a Summary
Les Murray, Australian, 1938–

The obedient Centurion whose slave is healed (Year C) sees the Sabbath-breaking healer Jesus (Year B) as a poet, and those who do his will (Year A) become his words, his poem.

That numinous healer who preached Saturnalia and paradox
has died a slave's death. We were manoeuvred into it by
priests
and by the man himself. To complete his poem.

He was certainly dead. The pilum guaranteed it. His
message,
unwritten except on his body, like anyone's, was wrapped
like a scroll and dispatched to our liberated selves, the gods.

If he has now risen, as our infiltrators gibber,
he has outdone Orpheus, who went alive to the Shades.
Solitude may be stronger than embraces. Inventor of the
mustard tree,

he mourned one death, perhaps all, before he reversed it.
He forgave the sick to health, disregarded the sex of the
Furies
when expelling them from minds. And he never speculated.

If he is risen, all are children of a most high real God
or something even stranger called by that name

who knew to come and be punished for the world.

To have knowledge of right, after that, is to be in the wrong.
Death came through the sight of law. His oldest
wisdom.

If death is now the birth-gate into things unsayable
in language of death's era, there will be wars about religion
as there never were about the death ignoring Olympians.
Love, too, his new universal, so far ahead of you has died

for you before you meet it, may seem colder than the favours
of gods
who are our poems, good and bad. But there never was a
bad baby.
Half of his worship will be grinding his face in the dirt

then lifting it to beg, in private. The low will rule, and curse
by him.
Divine bastard, soul-usurer, eros-fighter, he is out to
monopolize hatred.
Whole philosophies will be devised for their brief snubbings
of him.

But regained excels kept he taught. Thus he has done the
impossible
to show us it is there. To ask it of us. It seems we are to be
the poem
and live the impossible. As each time we have, with mixed
cries.

pilum – Latin for a lance or pike (which pierced the side of
Christ: see John 19.34).

78

PROPER 5

———◄○►———

He Was the Christ

John Shaw Neilson, Australian, 1872–1942

This poem celebrates the enduring love and compassion of the Jesus pre-
sented in the Gospels, who calls sinners, heals and restores, who knows
suffering for himself.

Our laws, the wisest, haste to die:
Our creeds like idle tales are told:
The loving heart, the lips that bless,
The shadowy centuries make not old.

This life, that ever runs to pain,
He felt it all; its rise and glow,
The bitterness, the ache, the toil,
All that the moving myriads know.

He drew no sword; but all men's swords
Grew redder in the blood-red years:
– Only the hope, that would not die,
Shone tremulous in a world of tears.

The white mist dances in our eyes;
But still, in every age and land,
His heart beats for the little child,
He writes of mercy on the sand.

PROPER 6

————◄○►————

The Kingdom

R. S. Thomas, Welsh, 1913–2000

This poem speaks of the strangeness of God's Kingdom proclaimed by
Jesus, which flourishes mysteriously like the mustard seed (Year B), a tree
of which faith is the leaf (Years A and C).

It's a long way off but inside it
There are quite different things going on:
Festivals at which the poor man
Is king and the consumptive is
Healed: mirrors in which the blind look
At themselves and love looks at them
Back; and industry is for mending
The bent bones and the minds fractured
By life. It's a long way off, but to get
There takes no time and admission
Is free, if you will purge yourself
Of desire, and present yourself with
Your need only and the simple offering
Of your faith, green as a leaf.

PROPER 7

————◄○►————

From *The Divine Lover*
Phineas Fletcher, English, 1582–1650

Fear is a theme common to readings in Years A, B and C. Fletcher's poem is a dialogue between the fearful disciple and Christ, whose perfect love casts out fear.

Me Lord? can'st thou mispend
One word, misplace one look on me?
Call'st me thy Love, thy Friend?
Can this poor soul the object be
Of these love-glances, those life-kindling eyes?
What? I the Centre of thy arms embraces?
Of all thy labour I the prize?
Love never mocks, Truth never lies.
Oh how I quake : Hope fear, fear hope displaces :
I would, but cannot hope : such wondrous love amazes.

See, I am black as night,
See I am darkness : dark as hell.
Lord thou more fair than light ;
Heav'ns Sun thy Shadow; can Sunns dwell
With Shades? 'twixt light, and darkness what commerce?
True : thou art darkness, I thy Light : my ray
Thy mists, and hellish foggs shall pierce.
With me, black soul, with me converse.
I make the foul *December* flowry *May,*
Turn thou thy night to me: I'le turn thy night to day.

See, Lord, see I am dead :
Tomb'd in thy self : my self my grave
A drudge : so born, so bred :
My self even to my self a slave.
Thou Freedome, Life : can Life, and Liberty
Love bondage, death? Thy Freedom I : I tyed
To loose thy bonds ; be bound to me :
My yoke shall ease, my bonds shall free.
Dead soul, thy Spring of life, my dying side :
There dye with me to live : to live in thee I dyed.

PROPER 8

———◄○►———

None Other Lamb

Christina Rossetti, English, 1830–94

Rossetti's poem might have been spoken by Jairus' daughter or the woman whose bleeding is stopped (Year B). These are the words of complete trust – the trust of Abraham (Year A) and of the faithful disciple (Year C).

> None other Lamb, none other Name,
> None other Hope in heaven or earth or sea,
> None other Hiding place from guilt and shame,
> None beside Thee.
>
> My faith burns low, my hope burns low,
> Only my heart's desire cries out in me
> By the deep thunder of its want and woe
> Cries out to Thee.
>
> Lord, Thou art Life tho' I be dead,
> Love's fire Thou art, however cold I be:
> Nor heaven have I, nor place to lay my head,
> Nor home, but Thee.

PROPER 9

————◄◦►————

In Church

Thomas Hardy, English, 1840–1928

That which is hidden from the wise is revealed to children (Gospel, Year A). In Hardy's poem a child sees behind the façade of ministry and 'church' to the reality beneath.

'And now to God the Father,' he ends,
And his voice thrills up to the topmost tiles:
Each listener chokes as he bows and bends,
And emotion pervades the crowded aisles.
Then the preacher glides to the vestry-door,
And shuts it, and thinks he is seen no more.

The door swings softly ajar meanwhile,
And a pupil of his in the Bible class,
Who adores him as one without gloss or guile,
Sees her idol stand with a satisfied smile
And re-enact at the vestry-glass
Each pulpit gesture in deft dumb-show
That had moved the congregation so.

PROPER 10

———◄◦►———

Stations on the Road to Freedom

Dietrich Bonhoeffer, German, 1906–45, translated by Reginald
Fuller and revised by John Bowden

Bonhoeffer's poem, written in prison, speaks of the rigour and cost of discipleship, and of their reward. Much is demanded of those who decide
for the gospel (Year A), who live it out through care of neighbour (Year
C), and of those who witness to the truth (Year B).

Discipline
If you set out to seek freedom, then learn above all things
discipline over your soul and your senses, lest passions and
      instincts
lead you now hither, now thither, in random directions.
Chaste be your mind and your body, completely subjected,
and in obedience seeking the aim set before them;
none learns the mystery of freedom with discipline lost.

Action
Daring to do what is right, not what fancy may tell you,
seizing reality boldly, not weighing up chances,
freedom's in action alone, not in wavering thought.
Leave aside anxious delay and go into the storm of our
      history,
borne along solely by faith and God's will and commandment;
freedom, exultant, will welcome your spirit with joy.

Suffering

Wonderful transformation. Your hands, so strong and active,
are bound; helpless and lonely now you see your action
ended; you sigh in relief, the right committing
calmly into a stronger hand; and rest content.
Just for a moment you blissfully touched upon freedom,
then, that it might be perfected in glory, you gave it to God.

Death

Come now, thou greatest of feasts on the journey to freedom
    eternal;
death, cast aside all burdensome chains, and demolish
the walls of our temporal body, the walls of our soul which is
    blinded,
so that at last we may gaze upon that which here is
    begrudged us.
Freedom, how long we have sought thee in discipline, action
    and suffering;
dying, we know thee now in the visage of God.

PROPER 11

———◄○►———

Cry of the Masses

D. H. Lawrence, English, 1885–1930

The Epistle readings for all three years speak of a creation transformed in
Christ, and this poem – like so much of Lawrence's writing – calls for a
reawakening of the bodily in an age numbed and enslaved by automation,
work and mass-media-led sensation.

Give us back, Oh give us back
Our bodies before we die!

Trot, trot, trot, corpse-body, to work,
Chew, chew, chew, corpse-body, at the meal.
Sit, sit, sit, corpse-body, at the film.
Listen, listen, listen, corpse-body, to the wireless.
Talk, talk, talk, corpse-body, newspaper talk.
Sleep, sleep, sleep, corpse-body, factory-hand sleep.
Die, die, die, corpse-body, doesn't matter!

Must we die, must we die
bodiless, as we lived?
Corpse-anatomies with ready-made sensations!
Corpse-anatomies, that can work.
Work, work, work,
rattle, rattle, rattle,
sit, sit, sit,
finished, finished, finished –
Ah no, Ah no! before we finally die
or see ourselves as we are, and go mad,
give us back our bodies, for a day, for a single day

to stamp the earth and feel the wind, like wakeful
    men again.

Oh, even to know the last wild wincing of despair,
aware at last that our manhood is utterly lost,
give us back our bodies for one day.

PROPER 12

The Bright Field

R. S. Thomas, Welsh, 1913–2000

The poet teaches that the Kingdom of God of which Jesus speaks (Year A), which he anticipates in his miraculous meal (Year B), and for which he teaches us to pray (Year C), is present among us in elusive and powerfully immediate ways for those who have eyes to see.

I have seen the sun break through
to illuminate a small field
for a while, and gone my way
and forgotten it. But that was the pearl
of great price, the one field that had
the treasure in it. I realize now
that I must give all that I have
to possess it. Life is not hurrying

on to a receding future, nor hankering after
an imagined past. It is the turning
aside like Moses to the miracle
of the lit bush, to a brightness
that seemed as transitory as your youth
once, but is the eternity that awaits you.

PROPER 13

———◄○►———

From *The Compleat Angler*

Izaak Walton, English, 1593–1683

Here the contented fisherman gives his version of true satisfaction, which
is to be found in thankfully accepting the sufficiency of God's provision
rather than trusting in the abundance of possessions – an ethic which the
Psalms and Gospel readings in all three years endorse.

Well, Scholar, having now taught you to paint your rod, and we
having still a mile to Tottenham-High-Cross, I will, as we walk
towards it, in the cool shade of this sweet honeysuckle hedge,
mention to you some of the thoughts and joys that have possessed
my soul since we two met together. And these thoughts shall be
told you, that you also may join with me in thankfulness, to 'the
Giver of every good and perfect gift', for our happiness. And, that
our present happiness may appear to be the greater, and we the
more thankful for it, I will beg you to consider with me, how
many do, even at this very time, lie under the torment of the stone,
the gout, the tooth-ache; and this we are free from. And every
misery that I miss is a new mercy; and therefore let us be thankful.
There have been, since we met, others that have met disasters of
broken limbs; some have been blasted, others thunder-strucken;
and we have been freed from these, and all those other miseries
that threaten human nature: let us therefore rejoice and be thankful. Nay, which is a far greater mercy, we are free from the unsup-
portable burthen of an accusing tormenting conscience; a misery
that none can bear: and therefore let us praise Him for his pre-
venting grace, and say, Every misery that I miss is a new mercy.
Nay, let me tell you, there be many that have forty times our
estates, that would give the greatest part of it to be healthful and
cheerful like us; who, with the expense of a little money have eat

and drank, and laughed, and angled, and sung, and slept securely; and rose next day, and cast away care, and sung, and laughed, and angled again; which are blessings rich men cannot purchase with all their money.

Let me tell you, Scholar, I have a rich neighbour, that is always so busy that he has no leisure to laugh: the whole business of his life is to get money, and more money, that he may still get more and more money; he is still drudging on, and says, that Solomon says, 'The diligent hand maketh rich'; and it is true indeed: but he considers not that 'tis not in the power of riches to make a man happy; for it was wisely said, by a man of great observation, 'That there be as many miseries beyond riches, as on this side of them'. And yet God deliver us from pinching poverty; and grant, that having a competency, we may be content and thankful. Let us not repine, or so much as think the gifts of God unequally dealt, if we see another abound in riches. When, as God knows, the cares that are the keys that keep those riches, hang often so heavily at the rich man's girdle, that they clog him with weary days, and restless nights, even when others sleep quietly. We see but the outside of the rich man's happiness: few consider him to be like the silk-worm, that, when she seems to play, is, at the very same time, spinning her own bowels, and consuming herself. And this many rich men do; loading themselves with corroding cares, to keep what they have, probably, unconsciously got. Let us, therefore, be thankful for health and a competence, and above all, for a quiet conscience.

PROPER 14

—◄◦►—

The Kingdom of God

Francis Thompson, English, 1859–1907

The God who is present to Elijah in his troubles (Years A and B) is present in Jesus, the rescuer (Year A) and provider (Year B), the one who says 'Fear not' (Year C). It is this same Jesus who is present to the poet in the familiar city, walking on the familiar water.

'In no Strange Land'

O world invisible, we view thee,
O world intangible, we touch thee,
O world unknowable, we know thee,
Inapprehensible, we clutch thee!

Does the fish soar to find the ocean,
The eagle plunge to find the air –
That we ask of the stars in motion
If they have rumour of thee there?

Not where the wheeling systems darken,
And our benumbed conceiving soars! –
The drift of pinions, would we hearken,
Beats at our own clay-shuttered doors.

The angels keep their ancient places; –
Turn but a stone, and start a wing!
'Tis ye, 'tis your estrangèd faces,
That miss the many-splendoured thing.

But (when so sad thou canst not sadder)
Cry; – and upon thy so sore loss
Shall shine the traffic of Jacob's ladder
Pitched betwixt Heaven and Charing Cross.

Yea, in the night, my Soul, my daughter,
Cry, – clinging Heaven by the hems;
And lo, Christ walking on the water
Not of Gennesareth, but Thames!

Proper 15

Fire in Stubble

Monica Furlong, English, 1930–

'I came to bring fire to the earth' says Jesus (Year C). This poem takes the burning field as an image of spiritual transformation.

Tongues of the Holy Ghost appear
All over the golden field
Pillars of sepia smoke arise
Tensed out by the wind like wool
Till the men half-hidden
Look like Elijah
Or like people in old photographs;
By nightfall the field is clear.

Lord, I long for your fire among my stubble.
You have had the grain, such as it poorly was
The empty field longs for your blistering wrath
It longs to laugh in the joy of your white-hot rage
To crackle and fall to ash on the dark-sweet soil
To be killed and born anew in your furious flames.

PROPER 16

————◄○►————

From *Experiences and Religion: a lay essay in theology*
Nicholas Mosley, English, 1923–

Here a distinguished novelist reflects on the ambiguity of the Church as
both servant and opponent of the gospel – the Church whose rock is
Peter, who confesses and denies the Christ (Years A and B).

The rules in one sense are that which have been found to give
framework, reference, order; that without which there can be no
freedom because there could be nothing to be free within or free
from, there could be no movement in a vacuum. But in another
sense they are that which brings petrifaction and death. In christian terms it is the church, the institution, that perpetuates (is the
manifestation of) the rules – both as life-giver and destroyer. In a
sense the church is opposed to everything a free man stands for: it
is that which Christ fought and which fought Christ: the denier of
truth, the torturer of the honest, the servant of mammon. All this
is too much felt now to go on about it: the concern of the church
for power, respectability, vanity, money – its obsession with sexual
morality and disregard for any other – all this, it is obvious to
everyone except christians, is just what stops other people being
christians and will go on doing so. But still, opposed to this, there
is preserved in the framework of the church (how else could it be
preserved?) the truth of the story, the history, the art, the secret.
The church is that within which the possibilities of the freedom are
held; through which is transmitted, beautifully, this experience.
(How else could it be preserved except in something so paradoxi-
cal?) Within the rigid and self-seeking church have been the things
that have given the chance to alter everyone.

Proper 17

---◄○►---

From *Piers Plowman: The Vision of Holy Church*
William Langland, English, *c*.1331–99

The New Testament readings for Years A, B and C emphasize that Christian love must be genuine and that believers should be 'doers of the word, and not merely hearers', for care of the poor is in the nature of the love which God has made real and active in Christ.

Love is the plant of Peace,   most precious of all the virtues,
Heaven could not hold it,   so heavy was Love,
Till it had of this earth   eaten its fill.
Then never lighter was a leaf   upon a linden tree,
Than love was when it took   the flesh and blood of man.
Fluttering, piercing   as a needle's point,
No armour may it stay,   nor no high walls.

Therefore is Love the leader   of the Lord's folk in heaven
And, as a mayor, a mediator   between the King and the people.
Right so Love shapes the law   on man for his misdeeds,
Love lays on man the payment due.

In thy heart's conscience,   in the deep well of Thee,
In thy heart and in thy head   the mighty Truth is born;
That was the Father's deed,   that formed us all,
And looked on us with love,   and let his son die
Meekly for our misdeeds.
And yet Christ willed no woe   on them that wrought him pain,
With his meek mouth   he prayed for mercy,
For pity on the people   that pained Him to His death.

Therefore I counsel you, ye rich   have pity on the poor,
Though ye be mighty at the law,   be ye meek in your deeds;

The same measure ye mete   wrong or right,
Ye shall be weighed therewith   when ye go hence.

Though thou be true tongued   though thou trade honestly,
And be innocent as a wean   that weepeth at its christening,
Save thou love loyally   and lend to the poor,
And share with him in godly wise   God's gifts to thee,
Your Masses and your Hours   bring you no more merit
Than slut Malkyn's maidenhead   that none desireth.

James the gentle   said in his writings,
Faith without fact   is nothing worth,
As dead as a door-tree   unless deeds follow.
"Faith without works is dead."

Chastity without charity   lies chained in hell,
It is but an unlighted lamp.
Many chaplains are chaste,   but where is their charity?
There are no harder hungrier men   than the men of Holy Church,
None more avaricious than they   When they are set on high,
Unkind to kinsmen   and to all Christian souls,
They eat up their "charity"   and grumble for more.

Therefore in the gospel   these words be written,
Give and it shall be given unto you;   I gave you all.
This is the key of love,   it openeth God's grace,
To comfort the sorrowful   that are with sin entangled.
Love is the leech of life,   next to our Lord,
It is the graft of grace,   it is the nearest road to heaven.

PROPER 18

---◀○▶---

From *The Growth of Love*
Robert Bridges, English, 1844–1930

This section of Bridges' poem is a prayer to the God who is Love, offered
in expectant hope which echoes the tenor of the Old and New Testament
readings given for today.

> Eternal Father, who didst create,
> In whom we live, and to whose bosom move,
> To all men be Thy name known, which is Love,
> Till its loud praises sound at heaven's high gate.
> Perfect Thy kingdom in our passing state,
> That here on earth Thou may'st as well approve
> Our service, as Thou ownest theirs above,
> Whose joy we echo and in pain await.

> Grant body and soul each day their daily bread:
> And should in spite of grace fresh woe begin,
> Even as our anger soon is past and dead
> Be Thy remembrance mortal of our sin:
> By Thee in paths of peace Thy sheep be led,
> And in the vale of terror comforted.

PROPER 19

———◄○►———

A Hymn to God the Father
John Donne, English, 1572–1631

The themes of Donne's poem – repentance, forgiveness, salvation –
thread through the readings for all three years.

Wilt Thou forgive that sin where I begun,
Which was my sin, though it were done before?
Wilt Thou forgive that sin, through which I run
And do run still, though still I do deplore?
When Thou hast done, Thou hast not done;
  For I have more.

Wilt Thou forgive that sin which I have won
Others to sin, and made my sin their door?
Wilt Thou forgive that sin which I did shun
A year or two, but wallow'd in, a score?
When Thou hast done, Thou hast not done;
  For I have more.

I have a sin of fear, that when I have spun
My last thread, I shall perish on the shore;
But swear by Thyself, that at my death Thy Son
Shall shine, as He shines now and heretofore:
And having done that, Thou hast done;
  I fear no more.

PROPER 20

---◁◦▷---

On *Another's Sorrows*, from *Songs of Innocence*
William Blake, English, 1757–1827

The values of the Kingdom reverse the conventional values of the world. Concern with status and wealth must give way to sacrificial service and faithfulness (Gospel, Years A and C). The humility of a child is to be a model for discipleship; in the powerless child Christ is to be welcomed and served (Gospel, Year B). Blake's gentle lyric draws attention to the powerful, compassionate God who 'becomes an infant small' and suffers with his creation as the 'man of woe'.

Can I see another's woe,
And not be in sorrow too.
Can I see another's grief,
And not seek for kind relief.

Can I see a falling tear,
And not feel my sorrows share,
Can a father see his child,
Weep, nor be with sorrow fill'd.

Can a mother sit and hear,
An infant groan an infant fear –
No no never can it be.
Never never can it be.

And can he who smiles on all
Hear the wren with sorrows small,
Hear the small birds grief and care
Hear the woes that infants bear –

And not sit beside the nest
Pouring pity in their breast,
And not sit the cradle near
Weeping tear on infants tear.

And not sit both night and day,
Wiping all our tears away.
O! no never can it be.
Never never can it be.

He doth give his joy to all.
He becomes an infant small.
He becomes a man of woe.
He doth feel the sorrow too.

Think not, thou canst sigh a sigh,
And thy maker is not by.
Think not, thou canst weep a tear,
And thy maker is not near.

O! he gives to us his joy,
That our grief he may destroy
Till our grief is fled and gone
He doth sit by us and moan.

PROPER 21

———◄○►———

From *The Plague*

Albert Camus, French, 1913–60, translated by David Peacock

In a plague-stricken town two unlikely colleagues, the atheist physician Dr Rieux and the isolated priest Fr Paneloux, witness a young child die in appalling agony. Their alliance is one of service in the fight against evil and suffering (Gospel, Year B).

Rieux turned round to face Paneloux.

'That's true,' he said. 'Forgive me. Tiredness can turn the mind and there are times in this town when my only feeling is one of revolt.'

'I understand,' muttered Paneloux. 'It's because this whole business is beyond our comprehension. But perhaps we should try to love that which we cannot understand.' Rieux sat up straight. Summoning together all the strength and passion he could muster, he looked at Paneloux and shook his head.

'No, Father,' he said, 'that is not how I see love. And to my dying day I shall never be able to accept a created order in which innocent children are subject to suffering.'

A look of anxiety crossed Paneloux's face.

'Ah, doctor,' he said sadly, 'I now understand what is meant by grace.'

Rieux had flopped back on the bench. Speaking out of the depths of his weariness, his tone was more affable.

'Grace is something I don't have, I know. But I prefer not to discuss that with you. The only thing that matters is that we should continue to work together on something about which we can be united and which lies beyond blasphemies and prayers.'

Paneloux sat down next to Rieux. He looked moved.

'Yes,' he said, 'it's true that you too are working for the salvation of humankind.'

Rieux smiled wanly.

'Human salvation is too big an idea for me. I have no such ambition. What interests me first and foremost is simply human health.'

Paneloux hesitated.

'Doctor,' he said . . . and then stopped. The sweat began to run down his brow. He muttered 'Good-bye,' and his eyes brimmed with tears as he stood up. He was about to leave when Rieux stood up also and with a thoughtful look on his face stepped towards him.

'Again, please forgive me. There will be no more outbursts.'

Paneloux held out his hand and said sadly:

'But I still haven't convinced you?'

'What does that matter?' said Rieux. 'You know full well that death and evil are what I hate. And whether you like it or not, we are together in the fight against them.'

Rieux held on to Paneloux's hand.

'So you see,' he said, averting his gaze, 'even God cannot separate us now.'

PROPER 22

————◄◦►————

From *Confession*

Leo Tolstoy, Russian, 1828–1910, translated by David Patterson

Tolstoy came to reject many of the formal doctrines of the Orthodox Church, which excommunicated him in 1901. Here he describes faith as a journey, a voyage towards God in which much is given and much risked (New Testament, Years A and C), and in which the struggling traveller comes to the divine shore, regaining faith in 'the life force' and 'will' which he trusted as a child (Gospel, Year B).

To know God and to live come to one and the same thing. God is life.

'Live, seeking God, for there can be no life without God.'

And more powerfully than ever the light shone within me and all around me, and this light has not abandoned me since.

Thus I was saved from suicide. When and how this transformation within me was accomplished I could not say. Just as the life force within me was gradually and imperceptibly destroyed, and I encountered the impossibility of life, the halting of life, and the need to murder myself, so too did this life force return to me gradually and imperceptibly. And the strange thing is that the life force which returned to me was not new but very old; it was the same force that had guided me during the early years of my life. In essence I returned to the first things, to the things of childhood and youth…The only difference was that I had once accepted all this on an unconscious level, while now I knew that I could not live without it.

What happened to me was something like the following. Unable to recall how I got there, I found myself in a boat that had been launched from some unknown shore; the way to the other shore was pointed out to me, the oars were placed in my inexperienced hands, and I was left alone. I worked the oars as best I knew how and rowed on. But the further I paddled towards the centre, the faster became the current that took me off-course, and I encountered more and more people who, like myself, were being carried away by the current. There were a few who continued to row; some had thrown away their oars. There were large boats, enormous ships, filled with people; some struggled against the current, others gave themselves up to it. And, looking downstream at everyone being carried along by the current, the further I rowed, the more I forgot the way that had been pointed out to me. At the very centre of the current, in the throng of boats and ships being carried downstream, I lost my way altogether and threw down my oars. All around me, in joy and triumph, people rushed downstream under sail and oar, assuring me and each other that there could be no other direction. And I believed them and moved along with them. And I was carried off a long way, so far that I heard the roar of the rapids in which I was bound to perish and saw boats destroyed in them. Then I came to my senses. For a long time I could not understand what had happened to me. I saw before me the singular ruin to which I was rushing headlong and which I feared, I could not see salvation anywhere, and I did not know what to do. But, looking back, I saw countless boats that were relentlessly struggling against the current, and I remembered the oars and the way to the shore and began to pull against the current and head back upstream towards it.

The shore was God, the stream was tradition, and the oars were the free will given to me to make it to the shore where I would be joined with God. Thus the force of life was renewed within me, and I began to live again.

PROPER 23

———◄○►———

Bitter-sweet

George Herbert, Anglo-Welsh, 1593–1633

In Herbert's poem to 'my deare angrie Lord', the severity of divine wrath and judgement, combined with the depths of divine love and comfort, become the pattern for prayer offered out of the ups and downs of life.

> Ah, my deare angrie Lord,
> Since thou dost love, yet strike,
> Cast down, yet help afford;
> Sure I will do the like.
>
> I will complain, yet praise,
> I will bewail, approve;
> And all my sowre-sweet dayes
> I will lament, and love.

Proper 24

---◀◦▶---

Prayer

Carol Ann Duffy, Scottish, 1955–

The Gospel for Year C urges persistence in prayer. Here the poet, writing in an age where faith has lapsed, hears the utterance of prayer in the sounds of ordinary suburban life.

Some days, although we cannot pray, a prayer
utters itself. So, a woman will lift
her head from the sieve of her hands and stare
at the minims sung by a tree, a sudden gift.

Some nights, although we are faithless, the truth
enters our hearts, that small familiar pain;
then a man will stand stock-still, hearing his youth
in the distant Latin chanting of a train.

Pray for us now. Grade I piano scales
console the lodger looking out across
a Midlands town. Then dusk, and someone calls
a child's name as though they named their loss.

Darkness outside. Inside, the radio's prayer –
Rockall. Malin. Dogger. Finisterre.

THE LAST SUNDAY AFTER TRINITY (PROPER 25)

———◄◦►———

The Ironist

Monica Furlong, English, 1930–

The Gospels for Years B and C present divine grace made known in human brokenness and need.

> Jesus, what an ironist you were.
> All your best stories were exaggeration
> And your best heroes crooks,
> To teach us how to live.
> What was it that you knew
> That made the cripples walk
> The blind to see?
> That death's the only way to get to birth,
> And brokenness the only road to grace?

BIBLE SUNDAY

---◄○►---

The Bible

Thomas Traherne, English, 1637–74

Traherne's ecstatic poem delights in 'the comfort of thy holy Word' and the gospel message told in Scripture: 'the blessed hope of everlasting life'.

That! That! There I was told
That I *the Son of God* am made,
His image. O Divine! And that fine Gold,
With all the joys that here do fade,
Are but a Toy, compared to the Bliss
Which Hev'nly, God-like, and Eternal is.

That We on earth are Kings;
And, tho we're cloath'd with mortal Skin,
Are inward Cherubins; hav Angels Wings;
Affections, Thoughts, and Minds within,
Can soar throu all the Coasts of Hev'n and Earth;
And shall be sated with Celestial Mirth.

All Saints' Day

———— ◄◊► ————

From *After Silent Centuries*

Waldo Williams, Welsh, 1904–71,
translated by Rowan Williams

Written 'For the Catholic martyrs of Wales', the middle section of this
poem (omitted here) mentions three of them specifically: John Roberts,
John Owen, and Richard Gwyn. Inspired by their particular witness,
Waldo Williams's verse celebrates the heroic living and dying of saints
who are joined with Christ's own sacrifice and resurrection.

The centuries of silence gone, now let me weave a celebration;
Because the heart of faith is one, the moment glows in which
Souls recognise each other, one with the great tree's kernel at the
    root of things.

They are one with the light, where peace masses and gathers
In the infinities above my head; and, where the sky moves into
    night,
Then each one is a spyhole for my darkened eyes, lifting the veil.

Oh, they ran swift and light. How can we weigh them, measure
    them,
The muster of their troops, looking down into damnation?
Nothing, I know, can scatter those bound by the paying of one
    price,

The final, silent tariff. World given in exchange for world,
The far frontiers of agony to buy the Spirit's leadership,
The flower paid over for the root, the dying grain to be his
    cradle.

Their guts wrenched out after the trip to torment on the hurdle,
And before the last gasp when the ladder stood in front of them
For the soul to mount, up to the wide tomorrow of their dear
    Lord's Golgotha.

ALL SAINTS' SUNDAY

————◄◦►————

The Alphabet Tree

Stephen Spender, English, 1909–95

Addressed to T. S. Eliot's widow Valerie, Spender's poem playfully celebrates the enduring words of departed poets in many languages, who
shine as stars in the ink-black literary sky. He calls them 'the more living
– the dead!' – a wonderful way to imagine the departed, and particularly
the saints.

Today when I awoke
Soon as dawn broke
I saw a ladder
Set up against
The Alphabet Tree.

From on high a Voice spoke
'Today you must climb
Up the rungs of this ladder
Each one a letter
Of words in a poem
That you must write
Rhyme mirroring rhyme,
And complete by midnight
When, from A at the root,
Heaven-reaching, your head
Through the darkness will shoot
To strike letter Z.'

So I climbed up A, B,
C, D, E, F and G,
H, I, J and K

(I was almost halfway!)
And then L, M, N,
O, P, Q, R and S
(Seven more to success!)
U, V and W
(Bets on me double now!)
Until I was up
At the Tree's dizzy top.

So I struck letter Z!
Proud, I then read
The poem in my head.
But 'Alas!' the Voice said:
'Your poem is a flower
Whose petals will scatter
On the breeze in an hour,
Zeroed by Zephyr
And unwept by Zigeuner
Zizzing his zither
Or twanging guitar!

'But behold where on high
The entire ink-black sky
Is diamonded
With stars of great poets
Whose language unfetters
Every Alphabet's letters
Interweaving through Time
In rhythm and rhyme –
Where the living shall read
The more living – the dead!'

Zigeuner – German for gypsy.

THE FOURTH SUNDAY BEFORE ADVENT

The Glories of our Blood and State

James Shirley, English, 1596–1666

For Zacchaeus (Gospel, Year C), the experience of God's love and salvation in Jesus is borne out in practical love of neighbour (Gospel, Year B). This poem asserts that it is the works of justice and faith which endure in an age where all else will pass away (Gospel, Year A).

> The glories of our blood and state
>   Are shadows, not substantial things;
> There is no armour against Fate;
>   Death lays his icy hand on kings;
>   Sceptre and Crown
>   Must tumble down,
> And in the dust be equal made
> With the poor crooked scythe and spade.
>
> Some men with swords may reap the field,
>   And plant fresh laurels where they kill:
> But their strong nerves at last must yield;
>   They tame but one another still:
>   Early or late
>   They stoop to fate,
> And must give up their murmuring breath
> When they, pale captives, creep to death.

The garlands wither on your brow;
    Then boast no more your mighty deeds!
Upon Death's purple altar now
    See where the victor-victim bleeds.
      Your heads must come
      To the cold tomb:
Only the actions of the just
Smell sweet and blossom in their dust.

THE THIRD SUNDAY BEFORE ADVENT

---◄○►---

Late, late, so late!
Alfred, Lord Tennyson, English, 1809–92

As the New Testament readings for Years A, B and C turn towards the Advent theme of preparation for the Lord's Coming, Tennyson's poem of warning and readiness takes up the parable in Year A's Gospel.

Late, late, so late! and dark the night and chill!
Late, late, so late! but we can enter still.
Too late, too late! ye cannot enter now.

No light had we: for that we do repent;
And learning this, the Bridegroom will relent.
Too late, too late! ye cannot enter now.

No light: so late! and dark and chill the night!
O let us in, that we may find the light!
Too late, too late: ye cannot enter now.

Have we not heard the Bridegroom is so sweet?
O let us in, tho' late, to kiss His feet!
No, no, too late! ye cannot enter now.

THE SECOND SUNDAY BEFORE ADVENT

------◄○►------

From *Seeing the Blossom*
Dennis Potter, English, 1935–94

Shortly before he died after a long illness, Dennis Potter, the playwright and television dramatist, gave an interview to Melvyn Bragg. In this excerpt Potter talks of what it means for him to know that he is dying: how the impending End leads him to treasure the present moment. Likewise, the readings for all three Years urge us to fashion a life which is lived in the expectation of finality.

I remember Martin Amis saying something about you reach your forties, your forties are middle age, and nobody ever tells you . . . what it's like. Well, it's the same about knowing about death. We all, we're the only animal that knows we're going to die, and yet we carry on paying our mortgages, doing our jobs, moving about, behaving as though there's eternity in a sense. And we forget or tend to forget that life can only be defined in the present tense, it is, and it is *now* only. I mean, as much as we would like to call back yesterday and indeed yearn to, and ache to sometimes, we can't, it's in us but we can't actually, it's not there in front of us. However predictable tomorrow is, and unfortunately for most people, most of the time, it's too predictable, they're locked into what ever position they're locked into . . . Even so, no matter how predictable it is, there's the element of the unpredictable, of the you don't know. The only thing you know for sure is the present tense, and that nowness becomes so vivid to me that, almost in a perverse sort of way, I'm almost serene. You know, I can celebrate life.

Below my window in Ross, when I'm working in Ross . . . there at this season, the blossom is out in full now . . . it's a plum tree, it looks like apple blossom but it's white, and looking at it, instead of saying 'Oh, that's nice blossom'. . . last week looking at it through the window when I'm writing, I *see* it is the whitest, frothiest, blossomest blossom that there ever could be, and I can see it. Things are both more trivial than they ever were, and more important than they ever were, and the difference between the trivial and the important doesn't seem to matter. But the nowness of everything is absolutely wondrous, and if people could *see* that, you know. There's no way of telling you, you have to experience it, but the glory of it, if you like, the comfort of it, the reassurance . . . not that I'm interested in reassuring people, bugger that. The fact is, if you see the present tense, boy do you see it! And boy can you celebrate it.

CHRIST THE KING

———◄○►———

Morning Glory, Starlit Sky

W. H. Vanstone, English, 1923–99

This poem, written as an hymn, comes at the close of Vanstone's *Love's Endeavour, Love's Expense*. The nature of God's love and power are revealed in Christ's kingship, who reigns as crucified Lord.

Morning glory, starlit sky,
Leaves in springtime, swallows' flight,
Autumn gales, tremendous seas,
Sounds and scents of summer night;

Soaring music, tow'ring words,
Art's perfection, scholar's truth,
Joy supreme of human love,
Memory's treasure, grace of youth;

Open, Lord, are these Thy gifts,
Gifts of love to mind and sense;
Hidden is love's agony,
Love's endeavour, love's expense.

Love that gives gives ever more,
Gives with zeal, with eager hands,
Spares not, keeps not, all outpours,
Ventures all, its all expends.

Drained is love in making full;
Bound in setting others free;
Poor in making many rich;
Weak in giving power to be.

Therefore He who Thee reveals
Hangs, O Father, on that Tree
Helpless; and the nails and thorns
Tell of what Thy love must be.

Thou art God; no monarch Thou
Thron'd in easy state to reign;
Thou art God, Whose arms of love
Aching, spent, the world sustain.

SELECTED FESTIVALS
AND
SPECIAL OCCASIONS

THE NAMING AND CIRCUMCISION OF JESUS (1 JANUARY)

———◆◇◆———

Unto Us a Son is Given

Alice Meynell, English, 1847–1922

This poem acknowledges the gift of the Christ-child as an eternal gift to the believer through faith, always being renewed, like the years.

> Given, not lent,
> And not withdrawn – once sent,
> This Infant of mankind, this One,
> Is still the little welcome Son.
>
> New every year,
> New born and newly dear,
> He comes with tidings and a song,
> The ages long, the ages long;
>
> Even as the cold
> Keen winter grows not old,
> As childhood is so fresh, foreseen,
> And spring in the familiar green.
>
> Sudden as sweet
> Come the expected feet.
> All joy is young, and new all art,
> And he, too, whom we have by heart.

THE ANNUNCIATION OF OUR LORD TO THE BLESSED VIRGIN MARY (25 MARCH)

—◦—

From *Magnificat*

Noel Rowe, Australian, 1951–

In Rowe's poem of five sections, Mary the mother of Jesus looks back on her life in the light of his resurrection. Among the strange and beautiful memories, her encounter with Gabriel, and with God the Holy Spirit.

The angel did not draw attention to himself.
He came in. So quietly I could hear

my blood beating on the shore of absolute
beauty. There was fear, yes, but also

faith among familiar things:
light, just letting go the wooden chair,

my knife cutting through the hard skin
of vegetable, hitting wood, and the noise

outside of children playing with their dog,
throwing him a bone. Then all these sounds

dropped out of hearing. The breeze
drew back, let silence come in first,

and my heart, my heart, was wanting him,
reaching out, and taking hold of smooth-muscled fire.

And it was done. I heard the children laugh
and saw the dog catch the scarred bone.

The Transfiguration of Our Lord (6 August)

———◦———

The Windhover

Gerard Manley Hopkins, English, 1844–89

As Hopkins admires the compelling beauty of the falcon in flight, so he comes to adore the glory which bursts forth from Christ 'a billion/Times told lovelier', who fills the whole creation with his light.

To Christ our Lord

I caught this morning morning's minion, king-
    dom of daylight's dauphin, dapple-dawn-drawn Falcon, in his
      riding
  Of the rolling level underneath him steady air, and striding
High there, how he rung upon the rein of a wimpling wing
In his ecstasy! then off, off forth on swing,
    As a skate's heel sweeps smooth on a bow-bend: the hurl and
      gliding
  Rebuffed the big wind. My heart in hiding
Stirred for a bird, – the achieve of, the mastery of the thing!

Brute beauty and valour and act, oh, air, pride, plume, here
    Buckle! AND the fire that breaks from thee then, a billion
Times told lovelier, more dangerous. O my chevalier!

    No wonder of it: sheer plod makes plough down sillion
Shine, and blue-bleak embers, ah my dear,
    Fall, gall themselves, and gash gold-vermilion.

THE BLESSED VIRGIN MARY
(15 AUGUST)

————◄○►————

From *The Paradiso*, Canto 33

Dante, Italian, 1265–1321, translated by Henry Francis Cary,
1772–1844

Cary's was the first of many translations into English of the *Divina
Commedia* (1805–14), and was acclaimed by Coleridge. In these verses
from the final Canto, St Bernard offers a prayer to the Blessed Virgin,
intercessor and friend of Christians, that the poet may be granted grace to
look upon the glory of the eternal Trinity.

O Virgin mother, daughter of thy Son
Created beings all in lowliness
Surpassing, as in height above them all;
Term by the eternal counsel pre-ordain'd;
Ennobler of thy nature, so advanced
In thee, that its great Maker did not scorn,
To make himself his own creation;
For in thy womb rekindling shone the love
Reveal'd, whose genial influence makes now
This flower to germin in eternal peace:
Here thou to us, of charity and love,
Art, as the noon-day torch; and art, beneath,
To mortal men, of hope a living spring.
So mighty art thou, lady, and so great,
That he, who grace desireth, and comes not
To thee for aidance, fain would have desire
Fly without wings. Not only him, who asks,
Thy bounty succours; but doth freely oft
Forerun the asking. Whatsoe'er may be
Of excellence in creature, pity mild,

Relenting mercy, large munificence,
Are all combined in thee. Here kneeleth one,
Who of all spirits hath review'd the state,
From the world's lowest gap unto this height.
Suppliant to thee he kneels, imploring grace
For virtue yet more high, to lift his ken
Toward the bliss supreme. And I, who ne'er
Coveted sight, more fondly, for myself,
Than now for him, my prayers to thee prefer
(And pray they be not scant), that thou wouldst drive
Each cloud of his mortality away,
Through thine own prayers, that on the sov'ran joy
Unveil'd he gaze. This yet, I pray thee, Queen,
Who canst do what thou wilt; that in him thou
Wouldst, after all he hath beheld, preserve
Affection sound, and human passions quell.

COMMEMORATION OF THE FAITHFUL DEPARTED (ALL SOULS' DAY, 2 NOVEMBER)

———◄○►———

The Lantern Out of Doors

Gerard Manley Hopkins, English, 1844–89

The commemoration of All Souls calls the dead to mind, in prayer and thanksgiving; we are one with them in Christ who, in the scheme of this poem, holds them perpetually 'in mind' – their Redeemer, friend and eternal life.

Sometimes a lantern moves along the night,
    That interests our eyes. And who goes there?
    I think; where from and bound, I wonder, where,
With, all down darkness wide, his wading light?

Men go by me whom either beauty bright
    In mould or mind or what not else makes rare:
    They rain against our much-thick and marsh air
Rich beams, till death or distance buys them quite.

Death or distance soon consumes them: wind
    What most I may eye after, be in at the end
I cannot, and out of sight is out of mind.

Christ minds; Christ's interest, what to avow or amend
    There, eyes them, heart wants, care haunts, foot follows
        kind,
Their ransom, their rescue, and first, fast, last friend.

CREATION
(HARVEST, THANKSGIVING, ROGATION DAYS, ONE WORLD WEEK, CHRISTIAN AID WEEK)

———◄◦►———

A Chorus

Elizabeth Jennings, English, 1926–

This poem is a celebration of God who is known in all the variety of his creation, and known also in human need and repentance.

Over the surging tides and the mountain kingdoms,
Over the pastoral valleys and the meadows,
Over the cities with their factory darkness,
Over the lands where peace is still a power,
Over all these and all this planet carries
A power broods, invisible monarch, a stranger
To some, but by many trusted. Man's a believer
Until corrupted. This huge trusted power
Is spirit. He moves in the muscle of the world.
In continual creation. He burns the tides, he shines
From the matchless skies. He is the day's surrender.
Recognise him in the eye of the angry tiger,
In the sigh of a child stepping at last into sleep,
In whatever touches, graces and confesses,
In hopes fulfilled or forgotten, in promises

Kept, in the resignation of old men –
This spirit, this power, this holder together of space
Is about, is aware, is working in your breathing.
But most he is the need that shows in hunger
And in the tears shed in the lonely fastness.
And in sorrow after anger.

Harvest Song

Mary Webb, English, 1881–1927

Mary Webb's pastoral lyric presents a blissful harvest scene which inspires a spirit of eucharistic praise.

The noise of bells has sunk to rest;
The low grey clouds move swiftly on.
The land is still as Avalon,
Deep-breathing in its sleep, and blest.

For us the holy corn is spread
Across the quiet, misty dales
Towards the hyacinth hills of Wales,
To give our souls their daily bread.

For us that starling flock took wing,
And, like a silken banner blown,
Across the rippling corn has flown,
To teach our spirits how to sing.

To Christ Our Lord

Cynewulf, Anglo-Saxon, late-eighth century, translated by
Sir Israel Gollancz

Here the poet implores Christ the source of all light and warmth to work
both physical and spiritual regeneration among his creation.

Hail, heavenly beam, brightest of angels thou,
sent unto men upon this middle-earth!
Thou art the true refulgence of the sun,
radiant above the stars, and from thyself
illuminest for ever all the tides of time.
And as thou, God indeed begotten of God,
thou Son of the true Father, wast for aye,
without beginning, in the heaven's glory,
so now thy handiwork in its sore need
prayeth thee boldly that thou send to us
the radiant sun, and that thou come thyself
to enlighten those who for so long a time
were wrapt around with darkness, and here in gloom
have sat the livelong night, shrouded in sin.

REMEMBRANCE SUNDAY
(VETERANS' DAY, ANZAC DAY)

————◄○►————

From *And There Was a Great Calm*
Thomas Hardy, English, 1840–1928

Hardy's verse was written at the signing of the Armistice which brought to a close the First World War, on 11 November 1918. He contrasts different responses to the destruction and waste of war: fatalist indifference with the questioning 'Spirit of Pity'. Wilfred Owen, the most eloquent poet of the 1914–18 conflict, wrote that 'the poetry is in the pity'.

There had been years of Passion – scorching, cold,
And much Despair, and Anger heaving high,
Care whitely watching, Sorrows manifold,
Among the young, among the weak and old,
And the pensive Spirit of Pity whispered, 'Why?'

Men had not paused to answer. Foes distraught
Pierced the thinned peoples in a brute-like blindness,
Philosophies that sages long had taught,
And Selflessness, were as an unknown thought,
And 'Hell!' and 'Shell!' were yapped at Lovingkindness.

So, when old hopes that earth was bettering slowly
Were dead and damned, there sounded 'War is done!'
One morrow. Said the bereft, and meek, and lowly,
'Will men some day be given to grace? yea, wholly,
And in good sooth, as our dreams used to run?'

Breathless they paused. Out there men raised their glance
To where had stood those poplars lank and lopped,
As they had raised it through the four years' dance
Of Death in the now familiar flats of France;
And murmured, 'Strange, this! How? All firing stopped?'

Calm fell. From heaven distilled a clemency;
There was peace on earth, and silence in the sky;
Some could, some could not, shake off misery:
The Sinister Spirit sneered: 'It had to be!'
And again the Spirit of Pity whispered, 'Why?'

Christmas Trees

Geoffrey Hill, English, 1932–

The ironic title of this poem is the name given by Berliners to flares dropped by Allied planes before bombing raids on their city in the Second World War. Living and dying in the 'Christmas light' of God's incarnation and suffering, the German martyr Dietrich Bonhoeffer represents a fortress of human dignity and peaceableness which stands against the destructiveness of dictatorship and warring powers.

Bonhoeffer in his skylit cell
bleached by the flares' candescent fall,
pacing out his own citadel,

restores the broken themes of praise,
encourages our borrowed days,
by logic of his sacrifice.

Against wild reasons of the state
his words are quiet but not too quiet.
We hear too late or not too late.

SOURCES AND
ACKNOWLEDGEMENTS

The editor and publishers gratefully acknowledge permission to reproduce copyright material. Every effort has been made to trace and acknowledge copyright holders. We apologize for any errors or omissions that may remain, and would ask those concerned to contact the publishers, who will ensure that full acknowledgment is made in the future.

Anonymous, 'Christ's Love-Song', from *The Faber Book of Religious Verse*, ed. Helen Gardner, Faber and Faber, 1972.

Auden, W. H., 'He is the way', from *For the Time Being*, from *Collected Poems*, Faber and Faber Ltd, 1976, with their permission and that of Random House Inc.

Blake, William, 'On Another's Sorrow', from *Complete Poems*, Penguin, 1977.

Bonhoeffer, Dietrich, 'Stations on the Road to Freedom', from *Letters and Papers from Prison*, SCM Press, 1971, with their permission and that of Simon and Schuster Inc.

Bowen, Euros, 'The Rowan Tree', trans. Oliver Davies, from *Celtic Christian Spirituality*, ed. Davies and Bowie, SPCK, 1995, with their permission.

Bridges, Robert, from 'The Growth of Love', *Poetical Works*, Oxford University Press, 1953.

Camus, Albert, from *La Peste*, trans. David Peacock and used with his permission.

Causley, Charles, 'Mother and Child' and 'I am the Great Sun', from *Collected Poems 1951–2000*, Macmillan, 1992, reprinted by permission of David Higham Associates.

Clampitt, Amy, 'Easter Morning', from *Collected Poems*, Faber and Faber, 1998, reprinted with their permission and that of Random House Inc.

Crashaw, Richard, 'Upon the Ass that Bore Our Saviour', from *Poems*, Clarendon Press, 1957.

Cynewulf, 'Ascension', trans. Charles Kennedy, *Early English Christian Poetry*, Hollis and Carter, 1952; 'Hail, heavenly beam', trans. Sir Israel Gollancz.

Dante, from *Divina Commedia* trans. Henry Francis Cary, Taylor and Hessey, 1819.

Dickinson, Emily, 'The blunder is to estimate' and 'Unto Me? I do not know you', from *The Complete Poems of Emily Dickinson*, Faber and Faber, 1968.

Dix, Dom Gregory, from *The Shape of the Liturgy*, A. and C. Black Ltd, 1945.

Donne, John, 'A Hymn to God the Father', from *The Complete English Poems*, Penguin, 1971.

Duffy, Carol Ann, 'Prayer', from *Mean Time*, Anvil Poetry Press, 1993 (New edition 1998), reprinted with their permission.

Eliot, T. S., 'Little Gidding' from *Four Quartets*, *Collected Poems 1909–62*, Faber and Faber, reprinted with their permission and that of Harcourt Inc.

Ellison, Ralph, from *Invisible Man*, Penguin, 1965.

Fletcher, Phineas, 'The Divine Lover', from *The Oxford Book of Mystical Verse*, ed. D. H. S. Nicholson and A. H. E. Lee, Oxford University Press, 1917.

Furlong, Monica, 'Fire in Stubble' and 'The ironist' from *God's a Good Man and Other Poems*, Mowbrays, 1974, reprinted with the permission of Monica Furlong.

Godolphin, Sidney, 'Hymn', from *The Metaphysical Poets*, ed. Dame Helen Gardner, Penguin, 1957.

Griffiths, Ann, 'I saw him standing', trans. Rowan Williams, from *After Silent Centuries*, Perpetua Press (undated), used with their permission.

Gunn, Thom, 'Jesus and His Mother', from *Sense of Movement*, Faber and Faber, 1957, reproduced with their permission and that of Farrar, Strauss and Giroux.

Hardy, Thomas, 'The Darkling Thrush', 'In Church' and 'And There Was a Great Calm', from *Selected Poems*, Penguin, 1978.

Harrison, Tony, from *The Mysteries*, Faber and Faber, 1985, reprinted with their permission.

Herbert, George, 'Discipline', 'Trinitie Sunday' and 'Bitter-sweet', from *The Complete English Works*, Everyman, 1974.

Herrick, Robert, 'To keep A True Lent', from *The Poems of Robert Herrick*, Oxford University Press, 1965.

Hill, Geoffrey, 'Christmas Trees', from *Tenebrae* (1978), in *Collected Poems*, Penguin 1985, reprinted with their permission.

Hopkins, G. M., 'The Windhover' and 'The Lantern out of Doors', from *The Poems of Gerard Manley Hopkins*, Oxford University Press, 1930.

Jennings, Elizabeth, 'Prayer for Holy Week' from *Praises*, Carcanet, 1998, and 'A Chorus', from *Collected Poems*, 1987, reprinted by permission of David Higham Associates.

Kennedy, Charles, a translation of 'The Whale', from 'Physiologus', in *Early English Christian Poetry*, Hollis and Carter, 1952.

Kennelly, Brendan, 'The Job', from *The Book of Judas*, Bloodaxe, 1991, reprinted with permission.

Langland, William, *Piers Plowman*, trans. William Canton, Everyman Library (undated).

Lawrence, D. H., 'Phoenix', 'Future Religion' and 'Cry of the Masses', from *The Complete Poems of D. H. Lawrence*, Heinemann, 1964.

Lewis, Saunders, 'Ascension Thursday', trans. Oliver Davies, from *Celtic Christian Spirituality*, ed. Davies and Bowie, SPCK, 1995, reprinted with their permission.

Longfellow, H. W., a translation of 'The Grave', from *The Complete Works of Henry W. Longfellow*, Collins (undated).

McAuley, James, 'To the Holy Spirit', from *Collected Poems 1939–70*, Angus and Robertson, 1971, with the permission of HarperCollins Publishers.

Marlowe, Christopher, 'The Passionate Shepherd to His Love', from *The Complete Poems and Translations*, Penguin, 1971.

Merton, Thomas, 'Song – If you seek...', from *The Collected Poems of Thomas Merton*, New Directions, 1977, with their permission and that of Laurence Pollinger Ltd.

Meynell, Alice, 'I Am the Way' and 'Unto Us a Son is Given', from *The Complete Poems of Alice Meynell*, Oxford University Press, 1913.

Mosley, Nicholas, from *Experience and Religion; a lay essay in theology*, Hodder and Stoughton, 1965.

Murray, Les, 'Easter 1984', from *The Daylight Moon*, Carcanet 1987; and 'The Say-but-the-word Centurion Attempts a Summary', from *New Selected Poems*, Duffy and Snelgrove, 1998; reprinted with permission of Carcanet, Margaret Connolly & Associates, and Farrar, Strauss and Giroux.

Neilson, John Shaw, 'He was the Christ', from *Selected Poems*, Angus and Robertson, 1992, reprinted with permission of HarperCollins Publishers.

Okri, Ben : 'African Elegy', from *African Elegy*, Jonathan Cape, 1992, reprinted with permission, and with permission of Random House Group Ltd.

Parker, Dorothy, 'Prayer for a New Mother', from *Complete Poems*, Penguin, 1999, reprinted with the permission of Viking Penguin, a division of Penguin Putnam Inc., and Gerald Duckworth & Co. Ltd.

Péguy, Charles, 'God Speaks', from *Basic Verities*, trans. Ann and Julian Green, with permission of Routledge and Kegan Paul.

Pope, Alexander, 'Hymn', from *Poems*, Methuen, 1963.

Potter, Dennis, from *Seeing the Blossom*, Faber and Faber, 1994.

Raine, Kathleen, 'Three Poems of Incarnation', *The Year One* (1952), from *Selected Poems*, Golgonooza Press, 1998, reprinted with their permission.

Rossetti, Christina, 'Passing away' and 'None other Lamb', from *The Poetical Works of Christina Georgina Rossetti*, Macmillan, 1904.

Rowe, Noel, 'Magnificat', reprinted with the author's permission.

Shirley, James, 'The glories of our blood and state', from his *Poems* (undated).

Smart, Christopher, 'Hymn 32: The Nativity of Our Lord and Saviour Jesus Christ', from *Hymns and Spiritual Songs for the Fasts and Festivals of the Church of England*, 1765.

Spender, Stephen, 'The Alphabet Tree', from *Dolphins*, Faber and Faber, 1994, reprinted with permission, and with permission of Ed Victor Ltd.

Spenser, Edmund, 'Easter Day', from 'Amoretti', *Poetical Works*, Oxford University Press, 1912.

St John of the Cross, 'Cantar del Alma Que Se Huelga de Conocer a Dios Por fé' (1578), trans. Seamus Heaney in *Station Island*, Faber and Faber, reprinted with their permission and that of Farrar, Straus and Giroux.

Steiner, George, from *Real Presences*, Faber and Faber, 1989.

Studdert Kennedy, G. A., 'At The Eucharist', from *The Sorrows of God and Other Poems*, Hodder and Stoughton (undated).

Tennyson, Alfred, 'Late, late, so late!', from *Poems*, Longmans, 1969.

Thomas, R. S., 'The Coming', 'The Kingdom' and 'The Bright Field', from *R. S. Thomas Collected Poems 1945–90*, Dent, 1993, with permission of Macmillan Publishers.

Thompson, Francis, 'The Kingdom of God', from *The Works of Francis Thompson*, Vol II, Burns and Oates (undated).

Tolstoy, Leo, from *Confession*, trans. David Patterson, W. W. Norton, 1983.

Traherne, Thomas, 'The Bible', from *Selected Poems and Prose*, Penguin, 1991.

Vanstone, W. H., 'Joseph of Arimathea's Easter', from *Fare Well in Christ*, published and copyright 1997 by Darton, Longman and Todd Ltd; and 'Morning glory, starlit sky', from *Love's Endeavour, Love's Expense*, published and copyright by Darton, Longman and Todd 1977; both used with permission of the publishers.

Vaughan, Henry, 'The Incarnation, and Passion', from *The Poetry and Selected Prose of Henry Vaughan*, Oxford University Press, 1963.

Walker, Alice, from *The Color Purple*, The Women's Press Ltd, 1983.

Walton, Izaak, from *The Compleat Angler*, 1653.

Webb, Mary, 'Harvest Song', from *A Mary Webb Anthology*, Jonathan Cape, 1939.

Weston, Jessie L., a translation of 'The Dove', from 'Physiologus', in *Chief Middle English Poets*, ed. Jessie L. Weston, George G. Harrap and Company, 1913.

Williams, Rowan, 'Advent Calendar', from *After Silent Centuries*, Perpetua Press (undated), with their permission.

Williams, Waldo, 'After Silent Centuries' trans. Rowan Williams, from *After Silent Centuries*, Perpetua Press (undated), with their permission.

Wright, Judith, 'Woman to Child', from *A Human Pattern: Selected Poems*, ETT Imprint, Sydney, 1996, with their permission.

INDEX OF AUTHORS AND TRANSLATORS

Index of First Lines